Colors

I0869392

jovis

Diskursiv No. 2,
Colors

Diskursiv (eds.)

jovis

Contents

Introduction
Andreas Lechner

> "I see your true colors. And that's why I love you." Cyndi Lauper (1986)

When contemplating the notion of "color" in architecture, do we genuinely wish to perceive its "true colors"? Is not color the ultimate Pandora's box, divulging far more than superficial aesthetics? Color traverses both the realms of objective truth and subjective taste, engaging profoundly with significant themes. By indexing various values—beauty, femininity, virility, vulgarity, queerness—color exposes the inherent snobbery in discerning these values within architectural contexts, alongside its numerous contradictions. For example, the chromophobic whitewashing accomplished by Western European myths of "purist" universalism starkly contrasts with the vibrant color theory courses at the Bauhaus.

Much like function, color is often presumed to pre-exist design, as if it were an intrinsic attribute of the product. This assumption fosters the misconception that design is about creating a spatial product, one that is conceptually resolved—such as "black on white"—and adorned with algorithmically determined trend colors. This perspective, however, overlooks two critical aspects: the city and the intricate process from design to completion. Both aspects are challenging to acknowledge within the constraints of modern attention spans and media formats.

The city, like any human living context, is not a product but a pre-existing entity, built with all its past, present, and future "colors." Despite this, it remains malleable, open to various forms of construction, materials, finishes, and atmospheres, whether familiar or striking, under both natural and artificial lighting. Thus, the "true colors" of architecture reveal that taste, social conventions, and money often serve merely to uphold a status quo—with all its implied snobbery, cronyism, and racism. Therefore, in our communication, we should strive not to gloss over the immense effort, hard work, and endless coordination involved in reconciling conflicting regulations, standards, and briefs—not to mention the tedium of detailed scheduling. By presenting only the edited highlights of our work, we undersell ourselves. Our "true" colors lie in embracing and showcasing the entire journey of architectural creation, recognizing the diverse contributions and challenges involved.

Of course, the central architectural question remains whether "... I am entitled to annoy others with my individuality."[1] However, as the panorama of this book aims to show, any appropriate answer must take into account a comprehensive view of the full design process. From an existing context, a brief, and a client, through to the built and perpetually evolving project, representing the "true" colors of our field is a task that demands more attention.

Notes

1 Hermann Czech, "The Work and Diction of Otto Wagner (1974)," trans. by Michael Loudon, in: *a+u Tokyo*, 7 (1977): 66.

Tool to Read, Tool to Write

About Color as an Instrument for Mapping the City and Interacting With the Urban Framework

Luca Tommasi

In a pivotal statement, John Berger affirmed that "drawing is discovery."[1] The act of drawing forces the author to "look at the object in front of him, to dissect it in his mind's eye and put it together again."[2] Often, if not always, a drawing is the final stage of a longer process of analysis, whose elaboration it represents: a synthesis, a *schema*. The Greek etymology of the word "scheme," as Vittorio Ugo points out, indicates "form" in a broader sense: not exclusively a representation of the constitutive rules of an object, but also an indication of its features.[3]

From the Latin treatises to the Renaissance manuals, from Durand's schematizations to Choisy's axonometric, we can recognize several methods for coding the representation and interpretation of architecture, whether built or imagined. By omitting the models of the "ideal cities" of the Renaissance (often coined as a reinterpretation of Vitruvius's guidelines),[4] we see how these depictions pertain almost exclusively to constructive elements and architectural typology—neglecting the analysis of urban morphology. The city is the place represented by the painters, or the map makers. The artists have different instruments with which to portray the city and, moreover, different aims. Instead, the representation in the cartographer's work is triggered by a radically different problem: the lack of technical tools able to convey the precision which is, today, requisite for any depiction of a city.

Exploring the meaning of the "scheme," Ugo encourages us to consider a deeper meaning of the ideogram.[5] More than an oversimplifying tool, it should be a reflection of the core of what it represents, a depiction of its genesis: a "theoretical drawing" able to act as a "graphical representation of a principle."[6] The Jerusalem Crusader map,[7] for instance, compensates for its technical lack with a depiction that is not exact but "theoretical" (in this case, also symbolic and ideal), a drawing that can represent the tangible elements and the urban ordering principles of the Holy City (Fig. 1). With the Nolli Map, the depiction of the city gains unprecedented precision: Nolli includes an additional layer of meaning, choosing a specific method to represent public spaces.[8] From this moment, after gaining appropriate tools to measure the city, its depiction will revolve mainly around the concept of the figure-ground plan.[9]

The briefly cited examples highlight how a (more or less) ideogrammatic representation can convey the principles of a city and its urban form. Nevertheless, the presence of color seems non-existent or irrelevant. If in the Crusader maps color has a purely ornamental function—as it does, strikingly, in the Egyptian depiction of domestic spaces and gardens—the black and white urban depictions are built on a mainly binary system. The contrast generated within these drawings renders a high level of clarity, but the map maker has only two elements at their disposal to convey meaning: the use of black and white thus leads to a drastic reduction in the amount of information available. When enriched by nuances or hatches, the clarity is sensibly diminished: the sharpness of the drawing becomes substantially different, leading to a less direct, less immediate depiction.

The evolution of ideogrammatic representations—as well as the growth in the use of color—has been subject to broad development across the twentieth century. These explorations, nonetheless, seldom overlapped. While certain crucial models—such as those purveyed by Oswald Ungers or Rem Koolhaas—always favored the dichromic cleanliness of white and black, color became a descriptive instrument (as in the practice of city planners)[10] for precise and extensive mapping, one that is hardly ever representative of the genetic factors of urban form and its design.

It would appear, therefore, that those city depictions which attain such theoretical intensity often opt to erase color, which is instead used in analytical representations. The city, however, is a complex phenomenon: one that, if faced with only two elements to represent it, could be portrayed incompletely. How can that phenomenon be densified in its depiction while keeping its conceptual sharpness untouched? How can a map preserve its clarity and, in the meantime, increase the represented elements? That's one circumstance where the inclusion of color into the equation may (re)solve it. To explore this solution, one can take advantage of the words (and works) of the masters.

As Mark Rothko affirmed: "We favor the simple expression of the complex thought."[11] To be precise, as well as maintaining density of information, a simple expression must derive from an intentional process. A process that avoids futile elements, by carefully selecting only those aspects needed to convey the foundational contents of what we are depicting—whether that's the city, or its architecture. Abstraction is the medium that can guide us through this route. This vehicle steering us along this arduous path is, nonetheless, an unreliable one, owing to its ephemeral and non-scientific nature. The etymon of the word "abstraction" stands, quite literally, for "dragging away."[12] Applying the concept of abstraction to a map means, after an in-depth analysis, being able to understand what elements are indispensable for representing a principle—and carefully magnifying them (Fig. 2). In an operative sense, it means "leaving out" or "pulling away" unnecessary lines, surfaces, and layers from a depiction. The only elements required for an ideogrammatic representation are the ones that have a structuring role, that stand for underlying principles. The ideogram, hence, has the aim of representing only the parts that conspire to define the structure of the subject.

Color, in this phase, can become an invaluable instrument. The choice of colors and the method of their employment is the key point. As already mentioned, the use of color increases the possibility of distinguishing different features. However, to avoid an exaggerated presence involving too many (or too many diverse) components, it is convenient to have a very limited palette. It is almost inevitable that the choice falls on the primary colors and their direct descendants. Red and blue, as well as green and orange, are the primitive elements, immediately recognizable and discernible. As Johannes Itten points out, referring to the artists of the Romantic and the Prime Gothic era, the "harmony of pure colors" achieves incomparable "effects that are simple, perspicuous, significant."[13] Itten stresses again—as Rothko did—the "simplicity" that is crucial to achieving an effective expression.

To represent architecture and urban form systematically, it is necessary to keep the tone and hues consistent, as well as what they stand for: in this sense, "the action of colors is to be felt and intended not only as an optical fact, but also as a ... symbolic one."[14] If neutral gray can represent a background, intended as the set of information needed to locate and represent precisely the place depicted (as it can be, for example, in the built context), red can be used to immediately recognize and stress the object of the ideogram—be it the object of the design or the analysis. Green and blue both possess an instinctive quality that can be traced back to their abundance in the natural world. In addition to the hues, this palette can be densified by adding (or removing) brightness to the tones. Colors can be made darker to highlight them (so as, for example, when showing a stronger value) or to show differences in the volume articulation. Equally, lighter and less visible color can stand for elements that need to be represented but are less important than others (Fig. 3, 4).

Color, in conclusion, can be a helpful (when not fundamental) tool. An instrument capable of pursuing different purposes but, at the same time, an instrument that enlarges and deepens our toolboxes when we are analyzing, representing, or reflecting on the urban framework and its architectures—already built or just imagined. Again, Itten invites us to reflect on the value of color and its instrumentality. Even if not directly concerning the representation of the city, one of his annotations referring to El Greco and Rembrandt becomes peculiarly significant here: color "disrobes his objective meaning to turn into an abstract component of the rhythm of the space."[15]

Epilogue.
LOBMYS. A compositive *divertissement.*

The method outlined here generates a bijective relation between the object depicted (the architecture, or the city) and its depiction: a relation which produces an interdependence between the two elements. Certainly, the object precedes its depiction, but this does not undermine the equality of this relation. Since color generates a fecund correlation with the spaces of architecture—and, in some way, it "learns" from them—it is not unlikely that (with a little inversion) architecture could learn from color's features.

Untitled is one of many classical paintings by Mark Rothko (Fig. 5). Painted in 1957, it is on display at the Washington National Gallery of Art. The painting contains three elements, but only two tones. Three different "fields" float against the background. The deep green of the two bigger rectangles clashes with the luminosity of the intense blue strip, which is enhanced by the presence of the darker, less saturated blue.

The painting displays two very simple features. To translate it, one must grasp the following traits. The first is the presence of two surfaces: identical in their character, in the substance which generates them; but different, as a couple of brothers differs from a couple of twins. The second is the presence of the blue, encircling the two surfaces but carrying its own peculiarity. The contour internalizes the two green fields, connecting them through a thinner, lighter strip: the thick frame accepts a smaller gift, whose brightening presence underlines—by contrast—the nature of the darker outline.

The open-air gallery will, accordingly, consist of two, very simple, features (Fig. 6). The first is the pair of courtyards (Fig. 7), identical in their uncoveredness as well as different. The precise molding of heights and proportions ensures they are equal in their diversity (Fig. 8, 9). The second is the vestibule. A covered path, a continuous serving space that faces its own variation: a mirrored stairwell giving light to this undivided path, an uninterrupted walkway cutting across the two levels (Fig. 10).

In the year of his death, Itten wrote in his diary: "As a word only related to other words gets her precise sense, colors reach their own distinct expression and their own precise meaning just in relation to other colors."[16]

Notes

1 John Berger, *Sul disegnare*, ed. and trans. by Maria Nadotti (Milano: Il Saggiatore, 2017), 3.

2 Ibid.

3 Vittorio Ugo, "Schema," *XY. Dimensioni Del Disegno*, no. 3 (1987): 21–32.

4 Marten Kuilman wisely compares nine "ideal cities" inspired by Vitruvius and designed in the Renaissance: by Filarete,

Fra Giocondo, Girolamo Maggi, Giorgio Vasari, Antonio Lupicini, Daniele Barbaro, Pietro Cattaneo, and Francesco di Giorgio Martini.

5 In this essay, the use of the word "ideogram" is preferred over the sometimes more familiar term "diagram." While the etymon of the latter means "to write through" and roots its mea ning in the representation of a phenomenon, the word "ideogram" is based on the "writing of the idea," thus standing for the representation of a concept or principle, more than the depiction of a tangible object.

6 Ugo, "Schema," 23.

7 Gustav Reinhold Röhricht classified different Jerusalem maps drawn between 1140 and 1321 AD. The so-called Crusader maps are clearly reminiscent of the Isidoran maps: the majority of them follow the model of the round map, and function also as a symbolic representation of the ideal city. In this text, we refer to the Cambrai map (the older, most distinctive map) and to the Hague and the Uppsala maps (chromatically and formally, these are probably the two most brilliant examples within the group).

8 While all the buildings in Giambattista Nolli's map are hatched in black, he picks out what he considers to be Rome's civic places within their floorplan, as if they were open public spaces.

9 Camillo Sitte's drawings for "The Art of Building Cities" or Allan Jacobs's same-scale depictions for "Great Streets" are notable examples of this method.

10 One could think, for instance, of the famous 1915 Plan Zuid, drawn by Hendrik Petrus Berlage, or the 1934 Algemeen Uitbreidingsplan, both for the city of Amsterdam.

11 Adolph Gottlieb, Mark Rothko, "A letter from Mark Rothko and Adolph Gottlieb to the Art Editor of the New York Times," *New York Times*, June 13, 1943.

12 The word "abstract" and its derivatives come from the Latin *abstractus*, past participle of the verb *abstrahere*. The verb, in turn, is an inflection of *abstraho*, from *ab*– (away from) and *traho* (to haul, to pull).

13 Johannes Itten, *Arte del colore*, trans. by Marta Bignami and Augusta Monferini (Milano: Il Saggiatore, 2022), 11.

14 Ibid., 14.

15 Ibid., 12.

16 Ibid., 8. Cited in his wife Annaliese's introduction.

Fig. 1
The Hague Map
Author unknown, circa 1190–1200

Fig. 2
Bijlmermeer, “synthetic” ideogram
Luca Tommasi, 2022
Interpretive drawing of the proposal
for Amsterdam’s Bijlmermeer
by OMA, 1987

Fig. 3
Bijlmermeer, “analytic” ideogram
Luca Tommasi, 2022
Interpretive drawing of the proposal
for Amsterdam’s Bijlmermeer
by OMA, 1987

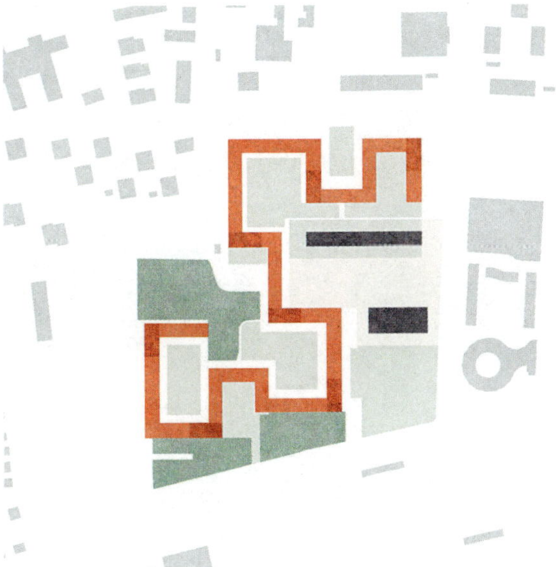

Fig. 4
Hoffmanhofe, ideogram
Luca Tommasi, 2022
Interpretive drawing of the project for Hoffman Höfe in Munich by Rapp+Rapp, 1987

Fig. 5
Untitled
Mark Rothko, 1957
247.3 × 207.8 cm, oil on canvas

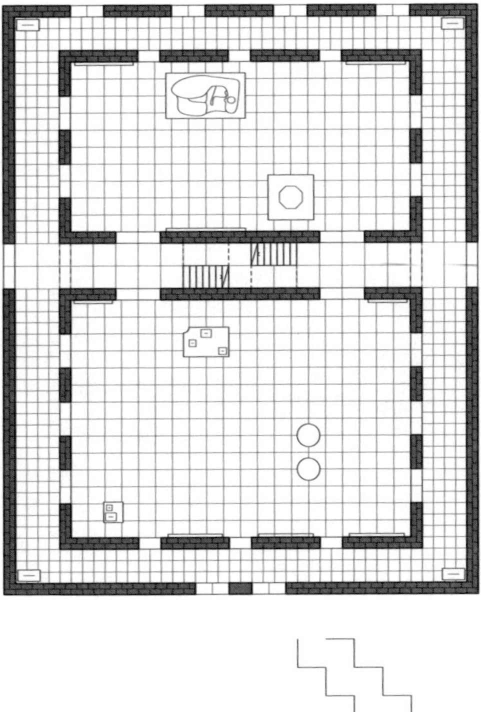

Fig. 6
LOBMYS. Floorplan
Luca Tommasi, 2023
Digital drawing

Fig. 7
LOBMYS. Longitudinal section
Luca Tommasi, 2023
Digital drawing

Fig. 8
LOBMYS. Through
Luca Tommasi, 2023
Digital picture

Fig. 9
LOBMYS. Low
Luca Tommasi, 2023
Digital picture

Fig. 10
LOBMYS. Above
Luca Tommasi, 2023
Digital picture

Schutzanstrich

Alex
Lehnerer

One day a stranger enters the town of Lago, a place sitting somewhere between the foothills of the Sierra Nevada Mountains and Mono Lake, California. Unsure whether this guy is a friend or foe, the paranoid townspeople peer at him from behind curtained windows as he rides into town. Soon after his arrival, the town learns that he can be of great help in defending against a group of outlaws threatening them. The citizens are so grateful they offer him absolute power. He agrees to help. Under one condition.

The Stranger demands that the whole town be painted red. He claims to see no other way to create enough visual consistency for him to defend the town against its enemies.[1]

The town is (literally) given a "protective" coat of paint. At first there is doubt, but soon the inhabitants are happily grabbing their paintbrushes. Everything is painted, from the bell of the church tower right down to the door handle. Absolute homogeneity. Nowhere does materiality seem to play a role. Instead, the only material property becomes the color red. What was initially a liberating sign of a new collective forming turns, rapidly, from an identifying mark of the group into a common performance and, ultimately, into a ritualized conviction and norm: the ephemeral color is now so omnipresent that everyone thinks it indispensable. Any remaining doubters are persuaded, with more or less pressure, to likewise paint their houses and possessions.

Cultural critic Dave Hickey describes how such light and laconic, though initially born of purely subjective expression, can become collectively oppressive.

He explains this using the example of the American artist Jackson Pollock and his work: in short, Pollock also enters the stage as a Stranger, with a technique as alien as it is new. He does not paint with his brush but drips the paint onto the canvas. What a radical act of liberation! Time passes and, at some point, none of the artists of the time can count themselves among the "contemporary" movement unless they also drip paint. The once liberating rule becomes a repressive one: "It's ok to drip paint!" or "Why not ... ?" suddenly becomes "You have to drip paint!"[2]

In the end it doesn't matter. The film's script (just like the art scene) is merciless, and the small town of Lago is overrun and burned to the ground by unscrupulous outlaws—despite all the red paint. Having the typical dilemma of any protective coating: it protects against outside forces, but also seals the inside.

Notes

1 Alex Lehnerer et al., *The Western Town* (Ostfildern: Hatje Cantz, 2013), 94.

2 See: Dave Hickey, "The Heresy of Zone Defense," in *Air Guitar: Essays on Art & Democracy* (Santa Monica: Art Issues Press, 1997), 157.

Fig. 1
Town of Lago painted red, secured in one visual move. Film still from *High Plains Drifter,* directed by Clint Eastwood, 1973

Some Aspects of Color in General and ~~Red~~ *Green* and ~~Black~~ *White* in Particular ~~1993~~ *2023*

~~Donald Judd~~
Marina Montresor

Fig. 0
Chiesa di San Salvatore al Vescovo,
thirteenth century

Perhaps because of my physical proximity to them, I am very fascinated by the beautiful color combinations of some of the medieval churches scattered over the vast territory between Florence and Rome. Their façades, made of green and white stone blocks quarried from the nearby mountains, were used as early as the tenth century in bi-chromatic patterns—usually in horizontal stripes—with famous examples ranging from the Campo dei Miracoli in Pisa to the Duomo in Siena or that of Orvieto. While these buildings are not drastically different from other "layered" architecture of the Middle Ages as found in other regions (different colors, similar approach), Florence seems to offer an interesting case: no longer simple juxtapositions, but masterful arrangements in which the horizontal stripes are replaced by geometric patterns suggesting something in between ornament and tectonic order. While the absolute masterpiece probably remains the Battistero di San Giovanni in Piazza del Duomo, I must admit to having a soft spot for the tiny adjacent church of San Salvatore, for San Miniato al Monte and, of course, for the Badia di San Bartolomeo.

One could say that Florence is a city of five colors, where most buildings are either made of *pietraforte*, a yellowish/brownish stone, or of two other combinations: gray stone (*pietra serena*) + white stucco and green marble (*serpentino*) + white marble (*carrara*).

"Pietraforte" literally means "strong stone" and its color and granularity always trigger an earthy feeling, further emphasized when the stone is worked as *bugnato*—stone blocks carved at different degrees of refinement.

The double arrangements, however, give a stronger artificial impression: while gray and white usually allude almost didactically to the dichotomy between load-bearing and non-loadbearing elements, the combination of green and white evokes a purely aesthetic desire, hinting at composition, tectonic order, and hierarchy. Green and white façades exist in a state of suspension between painting and architecture, or rather between the act of painting and that of building ... . Looking at them repeatedly and photographing them often, I always wondered what I could learn from them.

The epiphany came during one of my many sleepless (*sigh*) overnight train journeys from Vienna to Florence, while reading a text by Donald Judd: "Some Aspects of Color in General and Red and Black in Particular." Judd's lengthy essay got me thinking about these color combinations and what we could call the "problem with color" that most architects, myself included, seem to encounter designing (*and also dressing*). I began to think that perhaps there is something to be learned by approaching colors differently. Maybe colors can be considered as architecture and possess their own independence, much like materials, ornaments, and tectonic orders. Already in 1915, Malevich stated (and Judd quotes readily), "forms must be given life and the right to individual existence. Color and structure in painting are ends in themselves." Color and structure, color as structure, as material, as ornament, as spectrum ... . Anyhow, intentional color, that *must* be given life.

I therefore decided to isolate eleven statements (three is too few, seven too biblical, ten too absolute) from Judd's Notes and pair them with photographs I have taken of buildings in Florence over the years. These buildings may not always be the most famous or emblematic in an absolute sense; they were chosen only because of their specific relationship with color. Each pairing serves as a starting point for a brief reflection, aiming to integrate and expand upon Judd's statements, creating a landscape of possible interpretations.

This published version represents the current state of a potentially never-ending process of reordering, exchanging, and re-pairing. It might change later, but this is it ... for now.

Fig. 1
Leon Battista Alberti, façade of Santa Maria Novella, 1456–1470

1. “The necessities of representation inhibited the use of color.”

The builders, craftsmen, and masons who built these façades were masters at disseminating them with “evident secrets,” as per Johann W. von Goethe’s formula: secrets that are plainly available to everyone’s eyes, to the extent that almost no one sees them.

I’ll paraphrase one of Vladimir Nabokov’s *Lessons on Literature*, and say that when we look, we should pay attention to the details, and cherish them. I have no objection to the lunar flare of generalization, but only if it comes after one has grasped all the solar minutiae of the buildings.

In the Romanico Fiorentino, as in much architecture whose construction has been carried out by thousands of hands and minds, these details are everywhere, and they never decrease. On the contrary, they tend to experience a gradual, subtle increment. Like the kilim carpets from the Caucasus that passed from generation to generation and whose initial orderly, rational patterns were slowly altered by different owners. At every marriage, death, celebration ... someone would leave a small trace on the fabric: a personal symbol, a memento, a lucky charm.

Fig. 2
Battistero di San Giovanni, eleventh to twelfth century

2. “Every other generation has a new idea of color.”

When looking at pre-Renaissance—and therefore pre-authorial—architecture, projects appear less as objects and more as mythologies. By mythology I mean the collective repository of stories, regardless of their degree of reality, which speak of the same arcane figures but are subject to ever-changing interpretations. In Florence, before the Renaissance, architects were able to achieve orderly compositions through very free arrangements, where the totality has no parts.

They managed to create a narrative without any notable presence of form—or rather, they would combine forms and styles in a way that a chiseled and squared pillar can be put together with a round Doric column and a byzantine floor. Color binds the individual elements, but no part is ever subordinate to the whole.

By allowing for the dissimilarity of elements, they were able to preserve the identity of their distinct qualities within the whole, reaching the level of the system.

Fig. 3
Filippo Brunelleschi, Ospedale degli Innocenti, 1417–1436

3. “The red and black of the vase painting is color, the color of the frescoes is an accompaniment.”

I think I disagree with this one. I like the red and black Attic vases because it is very difficult to determine whether the figures are painted against the background or whether they have been removed from it. There is an interdependence that comes from the ambiguous hierarchy of the colors, which indissolubly binds the two as one.

As far as frescoes—and in general any figurative representation applied on a surface in space—are concerned, while it is true that often color is only a decorative layer, it is also true that it can determine space and confuse spatial hierarchies. In this sense, color is a space-making device like any other. Easy evidence: Rainer Werner Fassbinder’s bizarre choice of printing a gigantic reproduction by Nicolas Poussin which adorns the wall of Petra’s room in *The Bitter Tears of Petra von Kant*. The enormous figures become a lyric backdrop for Petra’s struggles, blurring the limits of the room both physically and narratively.

I like how in the Ospedale degli Innocenti, Filippo Brunelleschi introduces difference to the repetition by means of elaborate frescoes that hint at important moments in the otherwise identically repeated spaces of the *loggia*.

Fig. 4
Palazzo Pitti, 1458

4. “Color and space occur together.”

Palazzo Pitti is the first example in Florence (and probably one of the first in all Western architecture) in which the void in front of the palace acquires monumental dimensions to frame and leave space to the building. In a sort of *ante litteram* version of Mies van der Rohe’s Seagram, the large void not only creates space to look at the façade, but slopes toward it so that the walk upwards acquires an almost religious, certainly ritual, dimension.

Arriving from Via dei Pitti, one suddenly has the impression of slowly descending underground, as very rough stone blocks create the artificial ground on which the building stands and become the side walls of the street. Only slightly squared, just enough to be stacked on top of each other, it is impossible to tell whether they have been extracted from the ground or whether the ground has been excavated around them—only after having walked for a while and having lost the memory of the Palazzo, an enormous empty square opens up, sloping toward the entrance.

Fig. 5
Benci and Simone Talenti, Loggia dei Lanzi, 1376–1382

5. “[Johannes] Itten wrote in 1916: ‘Form is also color. Without color there is no form. Form and color are one.’ It never occurred to me to make three-dimensional work without color.”

Form and character (intended as atmosphere, impression, affect) are like heterozygote twins: while the former exists and is ready to be apprehended objectively, the latter needs experience and is volatile, ephemeral, and subjective.

In Venetian paintings color comes before the contour line. Everything seems vague and in perpetual motion. Carlo Scarpa used to say that the typical fragmented endings of the architecture of Veneto (the Italian word for them is *merlature*, and typical examples are Castelvecchio in Verona as well as a number of palaces in Venice) were made to mimic the dissolving effect that the humid lagoon air has on buildings. Where countless drops of water dissolve the light, forms disappear and only colors remain.

In Florence, where the sun shines and creates harsh contrasts between light and shadow, the contour line is fundamental and comes first—very neat, and precise. Colors are mere fillers.

In Venice, colors have an emotional impact; in Florence they have an intellectual one.

Fig. 6
Giorgio Vasari, Galleria degli Uffizi,
1560–1581

6. “Color should be part of the necessary diversity.”

The whole Renaissance period is disseminated with buildings in which “the necessary diversity” means the distinction between load-bearing and non-load-bearing elements. This is particularly evident in architecture using gray *pietra serena* and white stucco, but also brick and stone—I am thinking, for example, of Francesco di Giorgio Martini’s courtyard in the Palazzo Ducale in Urbino. In Florence there are many examples. I like the vestibule of the Biblioteca Laurenziana because it uses this distinction ... with a twist: *pietra serena* is used to create tectonic order, but also for decoration, creating a less obvious hierarchy and redefining the very notion of *necessity*. A less exciting—but, as always with Vasari, very obsessively and consistently realized—example is the Uffizi galleries... . I always enjoyed how the non-load-bearing statues are also white!

Fig. 7
Badia di San Bartolomeo,
1025; 1467

7. “I knew as a child that certain colors were supposed to produce certain feelings. I didn’t understand why a bull should be mad at red. Johannes Itten and [Wassily] Kandinsky taught in their important color courses at the Bauhaus that colors always produce the same emotions, and also that colors always correspond to certain shapes, the two together agreeing on the emotion.”

There is a big difference between an approximation, a description, and the more frequent oblique reference. In the *Romanico Fiorentino* color suggests fantastic order and decoration, defying gravity and preserving a unitary, flat surface. If the colors themselves were dictated by necessity (availability of stone, softness, and so on), their arrangement and forms were intentional.

White is the dominant color, but it only sticks out because of the green.

Fig. 8
Leon Battista Alberti, façade of Santa Maria Novella, 1456–1470

8. "[Piet] Mondrian's colors are one of the facts and wonders of the world; there aren't seven anymore. Perhaps if the four colors were equal in extent they would no longer belong to Mondrian. The preponderance of white to the bright colors is of course the determining ratio."

The long trajectory of green and white façades in Florence culminates—both chronologically and in terms of symbolic refinement—with Leon Battista Alberti. Namely, the Sepolcro Ruccellai and the implant of the façade of Santa Maria Novella.

The Gothic part of the church and the cemetery on the side were already built in green and white arches, so Alberti effectively let his design grow out of the existing arches. A gradual vertical increment in terms of granularity is balanced by a careful proportion between the horizontal surfaces. By preserving the coherence in terms of color, Alberti can use the same stones to update the symbols, ornaments, and knowledge embedded in the façade, and *the preponderance of white to the green color is of course the determining ratio*!

Fig. 9
Filippo Brunelleschi, San Lorenzo,
1421–1461

9. “Color as the spectrum and color as material, so to speak, are not the same.”

The uncompleted façade of San Lorenzo is devoid of any aesthetic intention beyond purely spatial and constructive considerations, resulting in the ambiguous perception of materiality and scale.

The only color is that of the material: rows of roughly-cut stones layered with a conglomerate of bricks and stones, slightly thicker and recessed. These setbacks, along with a number of seemingly random holes, were designed to anchor never-delivered marble plates and are now left exposed.

(Thankfully, our former mayor’s proposal to build a contemporary “interpretation” of the façade designed by Michelangelo hasn’t been pursued).

The uniformity of the color blends the materials together, thus contributing to the impossibility of apprehending the actual scale of the building from a distance: the closer one gets, the more granular the façade becomes, with the materials appearing smaller and the doors appearing larger.

The proportion of the doors in relation to the whole façade, together with the unassuming sloped roofs reminiscent of rural architecture, the large closed oculus, and the imperfect symmetry—all contribute to a surreal sense of scale. The sheer mass of the building makes us overlook its surroundings, generating the illusion that what we are staring at might be a big church or a dollhouse.

Fig. 10
Filippo Brunelleschi, Santo Spirito,
1419–1470

10. "All experience is knowledge: subjective experience is knowledge; objective experience, which is science, is obviously knowledge. Color is knowledge. As Albers says, it is very subjective, even hard to remember. Color is always objective .... Allowing for everything human being subjective, this is absolutely objective. Color as knowledge is very durable."

The absence of any solution of continuity in the *pietra serena* is perhaps one of my favorite things in Brunelleschi's churches. He does it in the Sagrestia Vecchia, in the Cappella Pazzi, in San Lorenzo, in the Ospedale degli Innocenti, and in Santo Spirito. While the floor grid evokes some sort of foundation, the binding of all the gray surfaces—which also correspond to the structural load-bearing elements—further reinforces the self-contained and absolute character of the space—a sort of infinitely looping system of forces and space!

Despite the criminal modifications made to the project after Brunelleschi's death, Santo Spirito still represents the surprising—and yet consequential—development of the architectural space as interior structure. The Occam's razor of the Renaissance: a perfectly symmetric and specular space, whose *pietra serena* elements frame the stucco. No frescoes, no further decoration. Freed from any ambiguity, the infill becomes fully spatial as it articulates into obsessively repeated, equally paced, identical semi-cylindrical chapels running around the whole church—yielding one of the most beautiful spaces (and floorplans!) ever.

Fig. 11
Badia di San Bartolomeo, 1025; 1467

11. “I wanted all the colors to be present at once. I didn’t want them to combine. I wanted a multiplicity all at once that I had not known before. This was very difficult.”

Hugo Riemann once wrote that “form is unity in diversity.” I always liked this definition which, albeit referring to music, also makes sense for architecture.

A repetition that occurs through difference.

A series of discrete parts that together form a whole and become a system.

Post Scriptum

Intelligent without being ordered, composed in old sense. Colored without or too small degree combinations, additions to final order.
Donald Judd, *Note* (1965)

Notes to the Notes

All eleven statements are taken from: Donald Judd, “Some Notes on Color in General and Red and Black in Particular,” in *Donald Judd Writings*, eds. Donald Judd, Caitlin Murray, and Flavin Judd (New York: Judd Foundation, 2016), 832–858.

All photographs were taken by Marina Montresor between 2020 and 2023.

A Space Which Avoids Color

Rafał Śliwa

> "Something red can be destroyed, but red cannot be destroyed, and that is why the meaning of the word 'red' is independent of the existence of a red thing." Ludwig Wittgenstein, *Philosophical Investigations* (1953)

We seldom hear about architecture where color is a space-making factor and architects rarely claim to use color for the achievement of novelty. Color is most often applied. What were the stances on color over the past hundred years? In 1914, writer Paul Scheerbart imagined a world that propels a visionary way of living. Structures full of light filtered by color were key to achieving it, which architect Bruno Taut attempted in first instance. The Glashaus Pavilion was opened to the public at the Cologne Werkbund exhibition in the same year. Scheerbart insisted in his text, "Glasarchitektur," that colored glass was a crucial element in construction of a new space. Alone, glass façades brought an excess of light which intensified a sense of social nervousness or unease. Color, applied as a filter, proved a potential solution. It could enrich the lives of the inhabitants and (re)solve the issue of social anxiety produced by the modern way of living. From the perspective of its own time, Scheerbart's approach did not attract many followers yet remained an important step in the discourse.

Almost a hundred years later, architectural historian Philip Ursprung and architect Jurgen Meyer presented *Cosmic Latte—Architecture Beige Manifesto*, making the claim for a new color paradigm. It was a retrospective reflection on the use of color in architecture, where beige was (re)discovered as the shade most often applied in the building industry. The phrase *Cosmic Latte* was first defined by a team of astronomers as the average color of the universe. Hence, it is rendered universal, as opposed to the revolutionary aspirations of white in Modernist architecture. In the closing statement of the manifesto, we read: "Cosmic Latte shows the big in the small—and the small in the big. It is a cosmology of the architecture of our time." It would seem that in the century-long hunt for novelty, the creative spirit of the age had landed on beige, and it is here that society found its content. There is still another way to look at the color, however—particularly by paying attention to where it has been evaded.

Avoiding color

Silver, known as a reflective tone of bright gray, has been regarded as a color since the fifteenth century at least. Its characteristic relies on the reflectivity of the surface which, in fact, could be applied to any solid color. It is a common property among metallic materials which vary in grayscale. When the environment rebounds onto a reflective surface, its base color is moderately concealed. The instability and motion, which are inherent to reflectivity, further displace the color. When such a surface is present in space, the reflections in movement keep our perception awake. At any moment the color of the surface is both one and many things, effectively becoming indiscernible and involving intuitive readings. Owing to the neutral base color of metallic materials specifically, their appearance becomes ambiguous.

The meaning of silver derives from the Latin *argentum*, which follows the proto-Indo-European word **h₂erǵ*, meaning shiny, glittering white. Not neutral like beige, nor radical like white, silver has acquired a more noble role in the past due to its value in the manufacture of luxury goods. Nowadays, its chemical properties are recognized in various industries and used for mass scale production. During the second half of the twentieth century, silver aluminum foil was applied on the external tiles of space expedition crafts, satellites, and equipment. It was a promise of "the future" during our parents' lifetime. Today, we can find it applied to cheap everyday products alongside expensive fashionable garments. Without reflectivity, colors like silver would be merely a shade of white or gray, depending on the material properties of the substance they derive from. But the intensity of reflection must be controlled since it has to absorb light in order for the color to appear—this is the crucial element for perception. What would it mean for space to be based purely on that premise?

Enclosed Spaces and Limited Light

One architect who quietly explored the characteristic properties of silver aluminum foil was Sigurd Lewerentz, both in his workspaces at Skanor and Lund (the Black Box), as well as the Flower Kiosk in Malmo Eastern Cemetery. The Black Box was his last workspace, a relatively small, dark, and isolated space, measuring only five by ten meters in plan. Lewerentz asked his companion, Klas Anshelm, to design this relatively private interior as an extension of Klas's home, where Sigurd was invited as a guest and spent the last five years of his life. It was directly accessible by internal doors on the ground floor, as if opening an entrance to another room, but it did not seem like a continuation of the old building. Due to its materiality, it detached itself. Little is known about the reasoning behind the formal decisions taken. The interior was dark, without windows, though it included three skylights and a small door at the end corner of the room. Perhaps these were the means intended as a way of avoiding distractions. Two of the long walls were black, made of asphalt-impregnated wood fiber boards. The short entrance wall was left in brick painted white, but the opposite one was covered by aluminum foil. The foil was visible from the entrance. One could assume a pragmatic use related to thermal insulation, perhaps preventing heat loss, but this would be inconsequential given that it was the shortest of the three external walls. What it created was the illusion of blurred, unending space.

Lewerentz also used aluminum foil in his previous *atelier*, located in the attic of his house at Skanor. From the photos we can deduce that its purpose could be related to thermal and lighting conditions since foil enveloped all the walls here. The way the interior appeared in pictures suggests something more, though. It seems to convey the idea of an introverted space where the foil's shimmer creates a

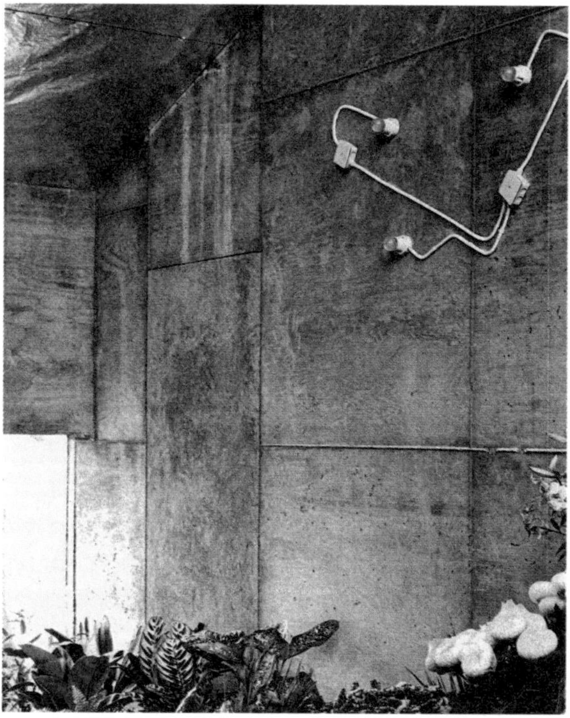

Fig. 1
Flower Kiosk, Sigurd Lewerentz,
Malmo, 1974

Fig. 2
Pavilion for the Kingdom of Bahrain,
Christian Kerez, Dubai, 2021

Fig. 3
Flower Kiosk, Sigurd Lewerentz,
Malmo, 1974

Fig. 4
Pavilion for the Kingdom of Bahrain,
Christian Kerez, Dubai, 2021

total sensation, filling the space with light from small windows. Another example is the Flower Kiosk in Malmo Eastern Cemetery. Two windows, set above head height, bring light into the space. Their openings intersect at the edge of a ceiling cladded with aluminum foil. The slope of the roof rises from the perspective of the entrance; from this sharp angle the foil reflects light, giving the sensation of extended windows. These two instances suggest that the use of aluminum foil in the Black Box could be a very intentional idea. Whether the decision was focused on pragmatism or not, it doesn't change the fact that this space appears almost uncanny in photographs, regardless of its historical context. Perhaps the use of material was a pure space-making decision. Lewerentz was known for his practicality and the versatility of his material solutions was a trademark of his creativity, likely stemming from the early craftsman's education he received at his father's glassworks.

In some sense, history makes a full circle to *Glashaus Pavilion* with the recent project by Christian Kerez, where light and color silently contribute to the experience. The Pavilion for the Kingdom of Bahrain at the World Expo 2020 is an enclosed interior, measuring thirty by thirty by twenty-three meters, dominated by a network of 126 columns. Their multidirectional placement tricks the mind into avoiding any attempt to decipher a structural rationale. The entrance is an enclosed corridor on a ramp that changes direction and descends, before opening onto the central space. The main interior is a public space for meetings and exhibitions, as well as a refuge from the arid desert climate of Dubai. The walls and roof were made of fourteen-centimeter-thin steel panels. The cladding—of 0.4-millimeter polished aluminum sheets—was mounted in a manner that included folding the edge which created an uneven, deflected surface. The internal forces caused by folding the sheet created the pillow effect of the aluminum. This enhances a sensation of movement and ambiguity. Columns were made of eleven centimeters in diameter CHS profiles. Naturally the gray of steel is darker than that of aluminum, and thus much heavier in its presence. Every column had to be intensely ground to achieve a surface that blended with the bright reflective tone of the aluminum sheets. Numerous tests were done to disguise the source material. Steel was ground until its base color disappeared, since "gray is a statement that one would not like to make," in the words of Kerez. Where the columns intersect with façades, thin slit openings appear, forming windows. The light is reduced. The tones of the atmosphere outside are gently reflected on the inside, filtered through windows covered by sand dust. The structure plays with the grayness of the ground concrete floor, which had local sand added to the aggregate. All this emanates a feeling of weightlessness.

In essence, the columns set against walls, ceiling, and floor were two dynamic layers positioned in unresolved tension. The familiarity of their surfaces generated a unified, soft aura which is hard to grasp in its nature. Their relation remained unresolved to the eye, since one could not determine its organizing principle, hierarchy, or sometimes even the perimeters of the space. It suggested a specific effect of well-balanced density and integrity. But the layers themselves wouldn't have felt so uniform if it wasn't for their color. The reflection on grayness of ground steel closely resembled the tone of the polished aluminum sheets and concrete floor. Two layers, so different in principle, were thus one and separate at the same time. This paradoxical affinity kept the perception awake, as the mind tried to decipher what's actually happening.

Avoiding definition

There is a temporal distance that separates the works of Lewerentz and Kerez, but there is also a less obvious familiarity that unites them. At the time of writing, the Pavilion for the Kingdom of Bahrain is being dismantled, or rather scrapped. It is no longer a space anymore, but rather an object in motion. The remains of its walls and columns reflect the larger surrounding, the atmosphere in Dubai. In this state of incompleteness, marked by a lack of enclosure and an excess of light, the idea of space is lost. The Pavilion only became fully active once it was closed, after completing the installation of the walls and roof panels. The space activated both layers: the pattern of columns and surrounding surfaces, in a well-proportioned balance between openings for light and the volume of the interior. Here is where the Pavilion achieved another quality, distinct from those spaces designed by Lewerentz. Scheerbart's arguments for filtering light or avoiding its excess echo in both projects, but without placing color at the forefront. Even though color is always there, each space escapes any straightforward reading of it. Instead, the attention is trained on the spatial experience.

At the peak of each decision lies the same question about meaning. For the above-described spaces, the answers could be left to our imagination. Perhaps the space that avoids the color may be the one that can achieve many meanings as much as the one that represents none.

I am grateful to Bartosz Bukowski, the project leader of the Pavilion for the Kingdom of Bahrain at Christian Kerez's office. Without his generous insights during many conversations about the Pavilion, this text wouldn't appear in the present form.

Flecks of Color

Tabea Marschall and Elise Limon

This text is co-authored by two people, who—through their respective educational backgrounds—have been designated artist and architect. If we were asked to reduce what we "do" to a succinct label, this might be our description too. Yet, we know that the boundaries between these two disciplines are not easily demarcated. They blur. It is their proximity and overlap that we find an interesting site to consider as two collaborators, two friends. We use color as a subject through which to tease out the nuances of this hazy disciplinary zone.

One way color is concretized, its elusiveness pinned down in order to be passed around, is through naming. Visual memory functions very differently to auditory memory. As quickly as we perceive colors, they disappear again. Despite the seemingly endless ways to classify color—through both common and more obscure terms, including Hex color, PMS, RGB, CMYK—our daily vocabulary falls back on clunky signifiers. Red – Green. Blue – Pink. Black – White. In this text, we move between these broad markers, our own perceptions, feelings, and acquired knowledge. Taking it in turn to consider a color, in a kind of correspondence, we wander through references, approaching color so as to develop more of an eye for it. As a form of training, we use color as a lens—a method of seeing or noticing—rehearsing its articulation in relation to both of our practices.

Pink/Purple, Blue, Green by Tabea Marschall
Color/No-Color, Red, Chartreuse by Elise Limon

Color/No-Color

The tutors I have encountered while studying architecture could be sorted into two categories. Those that encouraged a playfulness with color in projects, and those that challenged us to work without it. In my education, they generally came one after the other. In the second year of architecture school, color was practically forbidden. Everything was to be rendered with a thin black line, appropriately weighted, 0.05pt, 0.09pt, 0.13pt, maybe 0.35pt for a thick ground line. We were rehearsing resolution and clarity. Color supposedly muddied these aspirations. I learned "Pure Black" was not, in fact, actually black. "Registration Black" was black. The lines were as fine as a needle, but their shade mattered. We were striving for some kind of purity. Precision? Exceptions were made for extremely detailed drawings, where background information, finely drafted, could have its 0.05pt stroke rendered in a gray-tone. Everything was subtle. Color was considered suspicious. Had you really thought about its selection? Its meaning was heavy; we were to master black and white first, since everything else was merely distraction.

Paul Klee, who thought a lot about color, once wrote in his diary: "I still come closest to success with drawing. When I use color the results are more dubious."[1] It is true that there are more variables when you introduce color. It becomes a game of balance.

In the final year, the ban was lifted—all shades were accessible again. The architecture I made changed. Incorporating color was accompanied by an attitude shift. Multiple, messy, hybrid. The buildings and their shades were designed to encourage joyfulness, to embody "diversity, heterogeneity, and a capacity for mash-up," to be "unhygienic, unpolished." Color wasn't questioned. Color still had meaning; it could be an analytical lens as well as a propositional toy. We learned to read the city of Sheffield through its red-brick and silver-steel. The shades, which moved from brown to orange to red, gave us clues about how the built fabric was assembled from this particular landscape: its geology, its ores, and the industry the city eventually cradled between its valleys. We presented architecture. A reference, *Castle and Sun* by Paul Klee, was gifted to us in return. What do you learn from a painting, in order to think about architecture?

We were shown Giorgio Morandi and told: "Make buildings like Morandi." I am still trying to work out what this means.

Blue

I have never painted, but in my first year at the Berlin University of the Arts we were given a rough overview of the supposed history of art. We would stand in front of paintings for hours and slowly learn how to see. Blue always seemed to open up a distance, until I saw the *Blue Boy* by Thomas Gainsborough. Painted around 1770, it encapsulates a lot of information about Gainsborough's approach to painting—through his depiction of a young boy dressed in a light blue robe, he demonstrates his finest technical skill. The *Blue Boy* has become quite famous and has hung in several museums across Europe, his robe shimmering. He appears gentle, the aloofness of the shade blue having seemingly disappeared. The style of the painting—the robe, the composition—is a reference to a young boy painted years before by Anthony van Dyck.[2] Dyck's boy wore flaming red.

In painting, red usually seems closer and blue further away. Distant objects and landscapes are often blurred and kept in cool tones, tones that shift closer toward black. For me, it is blue that most strongly illustrates spatiality and at the same time raises questions. It seems to be boundless, like when it tinges the sky or the sea. And yet, it meets me with an intimate warmth in the writing of Maggie Nelson. Her book *Bluets* seems a very personal, complicated declaration of her love for the color blue. There, I read: "I'm trying to talk about what blue means, or what it means to me, apart from the meaning." And a few pages further on: "There are no instruments for measuring color, there are no 'color thermometers.' How could there be, as 'color knowledge' always remains contingent upon an individual perceiver?"[3] Blue has a depth, a suggestive depth. The suspension of blue in the emptiness of space—like the other side of the sky.

What does the blue of the sky do to architecture and space? I am standing in front of the Mies van der Rohe building of the Neue Nationalgalerie in Berlin, thinking about these questions.

Currently on show are the works of the artist Monica Bonvicini, my former professor. A huge surface composed of mirrors obscures much of the frontal view of the building. The mirrored surface leans casually against the protruding roof at a slight angle in a lascivious gesture. In large letters, partly cut off, are three words: "I do you." From my position, I catch sight of the sky on the mirrored surface, blue mixed with the soft white-gray clouds. The sky opens up a boundless space, the blue symbolizes that indefinable and infinite space. Do the mirrors and their collusion with the sky address a limitedness in architecture? Is this a gesture against architecture, in that it partially covers it up in order to reveal a much larger space?

I read in an interview with the artist that she often imagines what it would be like if there were no buildings, if the power struggles produced and reproduced by the built environments were to simply disappear.[4] I like the moving gaze that her work animates, a constant movement between interior and exterior space folding them together. And yet the huge "I" on it almost seems to crush me. I move further and further away from the blue as time passes by and twilight falls. The black of the letters brings a darkness closer. Do all colors disappear through an emerging black? Does the color space dissolve in the darkness?

Darkness occurs when light becomes dimmer and bright light activates the color receptors (cones) in the retinas. In twilight, on the other hand, the cones are only sensitive to brightness. This causes colors to disappear, leaving primarily contours, shapes, lines, and surfaces to stand out. Now, standing in front of the Neue Nationalgalerie at dusk, the artist's work combines with the architect's building, both becoming just one outline.

Pink/Purple

Recently, I spent a few days in a white, twenty-two-square-meter room with a slightly vaulted ceiling. It is on the ground floor, has a large window, and glass door facing the street. This is the exhibition space in which I am currently setting up my work.

To escape all this white space, I think a lot about light. There are four LED fluorescent tubes on the ceiling and, as it is already November, it will be dark during the space's opening hours. I brought color foils—mainly used in theater and film—with me for the set-up. I have two different colors, Cornflower and CTO+—the first a kind of darker, sandy orange and the second an almost-violet, deep blue. I wrap two of the LED tubes in one foil and two in the other one. I wanted to install only one color, but I found the two colors combine to produce interesting gradients in the room. Together they create flowing transitions toward a pink/violet tone. Sometimes it feels warming, and on the other hand, it cools. You move through the room toward different light sources and thus also toward their associated sensations and perceptions. I find it particularly exciting to look into the room from the outside. From here the color gradient appears again transformed: it is now cooler, shifting in response to the dark surroundings of the street.

The question of space and color appeals to me. A spatial organization of color takes place in paintings. Is this room I am creating a painting? Colors are placed above or below each other, in front of or behind each other. Boundaries of color are created by softness, while harder boundaries make the colors feel distant, separated. They read as here and there, above and beyond, there and there. Hues appear temporarily placed, directed from before to now, from now to after. Despite being composed of different shades, color assumes a coherence in one space. As long as it remains, we can return to it again and again, perceiving it in many different ways.

Red

Architects struggle to get through a presentation without showing a map, usually at a scale of 1:500 or so, on which a red outline obediently encircles a patch of land, deemed "The Site." It is within this perimeter that the architect will meddle. Within this perimeter, information appears; outside it, context often evaporates.

Private property inscribes legal limits to land; thus the red line assumes an obstinate presence. It delimits—in service of a design profession that has scarce time, scarce funding, scarce attention—a realm of responsibility. We know better. The red line is a representation, as is the legal land plot. Interventions do not obey such borders. Matter travels in and out. I am against red lines.

Green

The problem with green is that it is transient. It is like a guest—fleeting, flowing, swaying back and forth. Green begs to be referred to in terms of a "natural" color spectrum that

I immediately want to disregard to consider artificial spaces, to move toward the green screen. Green or blue backgrounds are replaced with videos or photos, a visual effect in which chrominance is used to cut out visual material. In film cameras, one pixel consists of one red and blue pixel and two green pixels each. This means there is twice as much image information for green, which makes it particularly suitable for video shots. If a person is in front of a large green screen, they can be distinguished from the background very precisely. Green is a tone that occurs only very slightly in the skin colors of most people, not in the same way as red and blue.

If one were completely green, however, one could disappear in digital images. In the video work *How Not to Be Seen: A Fucking Didactic Educational .MOV* file by Hito Steyerl, she deals with contemporary conditions of virtual representation and omnipresent surveillance through images.[5] The video work is divided into five lessons on how to become invisible in a world of images. Gliding out of the artist's photo studio and the set-up green screen, the video takes us through animated renderings of generic architectural spaces (shopping malls, hotels, resorts, etc., what Koolhaas terms "junkspaces").[6] Virtual and real spaces merge. Steyerl tries to develop new choreographies as countermeasures to these and suggests becoming invisible through playful gestures. Digital formats and specific transitive actions provide access to information while reinforcing structures of control. Invisibility in this context can be understood as a political stance, a kind of resistance. Hito Steyerl offers two possibilities of active critique: fight or destruction.

The video ends with people in green full-body suits beating a blackboard with their fists. On the board is an image of a real place: a patch of marked gray concrete in the Californian desert, once used by the U.S. Air Force to calibrate its surveillance cameras. It is an act of sabotage and can thus be read not as a counterpart to the call to retreat, but as a call to destruction. Green as a way to disappear.

Chartreuse

On the train from New Haven to Grand Central Station I pass through the distinctive New England marshes. The tracks trace a line along one side of the Long Island Sound. It is November and the patina of the saltwater marshes tells the time. Their fine tufts are a wintery orange brown, not green. Martin Johnson Heade painted these marshes, flat stretches of landscape, with marsh hay raggedly assembled into piles. John Stilgoe said we lost the marshes when we stopped painting them and began photographing them.[7] The peculiar way light treats these grasses at different times of the year was captured in the soft contrasts, the yellow and white paint Heade used. He painted the colors one experienced.

In 1999, Kodak released a memo titled "Why a Color May Not Reproduce Correctly." It stated that some colors may not reproduce properly on their latest films. These colors—"chartreuse, lime, pink, and orange"—Stilgoe observes, are the colors of the littoral edge. A site where salty water and emerging ground mix together to produce a particular palette of colors. In the alchemy of film, they would be distorted.

Kodak admitted in this memo that: "... a film could be designed that would reproduce these colors better, but then some of the more important colors would suffer." In spring, the salt-water marshes are an intense chartreuse, almost neon in the daylight.

If our understanding of place is structured by the representations of it, what would it mean to lose a sense of its color? Does this affect its value? To see it in black and white film instead of the brightness of oils on canvas. Mediums that produce and reproduce perception.

Ludwig Wittgenstein advises not simply looking at the colors in nature in order to understand them, because "looking teaches us nothing about the concepts of color."[8] Through approaching surfaces, light, forms, and sensations, we perhaps come closer to defining blue, red, green, pink, purple, chartreuse, but still we remain at adistance, always skirting the perimeter of their "true" meanings. A real grasp is elusive, maybe even impossible. Is our visual understanding entirely limited to our own being, then? Our individual perception, thinking, and feeling? Reflecting further on our collaboration/correspondence, we are struck by the echo of Frank Stella's statement: "Thinking about color abstractly hasn't done me any good."[9]

Notes

1 Paul Klee, *The Diaries of Paul Klee, 1898–1918*, (University of California Press: 1964).
2 Maggie Nelson, *Bluets* (Seattle: Wave Books, 2009), 16.
3 Nelson, *Bluets*, 39.
4 Jennifer Allen in an interview with Monica Bonvicini. See "You have something under your bed and something over your head. And you need both," in *spike*, 2004, accessed December 15, 2022, https://spikeartmagazine.com/?q=articles/monica-bonvicini-you-have-something-under-your-belt-and-something-over-your-head-and-you.
5 Hito Steyerl, *How not to be seen: a fucking didactic educational. MOV file* (2013), seen at https://www.youtube.com/watch?v=LE3RlrVEyuo.
6 Tom Holert, "Was baust du? Hito Steyerl und die Beweglichkeit der Konfiguration," in Hito Steyerl, *I will survive* (Leipzig: Spector Books, 2020), 36.
7 John R. Stilgoe, *Alongshore* (New Haven: Yale University Press, 1994).
8 Ludwig Wittgenstein, *Remarks on Color* (Oxford: Blackwell, 1977).
9 John Berger, *I Send You This Cadmium Red: A Correspondence between John Berger and John Christie* (Barcelona: Actar, 2000).

I Live in the House With the Blue Roof

Nikola Hergovich

I studied architecture at TU Vienna. Simultaneously I taught myself how to take photographs. I see myartistic work as a blend of different interests and disciplines—often but not only operating in the field of architecture.

Initially, photography was an extension of my architectural practice, a means of enriching my discussion with the environment and my surroundings. Later it became its own praxis, which can be treated separately. I mostly shoot on 35mm color film.

Today I'm interested in my direct ambience. Sometimes I include personal reference. Sometimes the images function as a note or a reminder. I like non-moving objects and ordinary places as well as fleeting places and atmosphere, which may be gone soon.

When I think of color in an architectural context I have a strong memory of my childhood neighbor. A girl the same age, living in the same street. I grew up in a small town in Burgenland next to the Hungarian border. She was my best friend and I wanted to visit her as much as possible. Every house looked almost the same. Normal houses with gable roofs and gardens. I was still really young, and I often struggled to find her house. One day she told me: "Hey Niko, I live in the house with the blue roof." From then on everything was clear to me. I could find her every time.

I spent a lot of time with her and her family. Her father was a construction worker. Now and again, when I came by, he would have changed something on their property. He'd built a new wall. He'd put a hole in the wall. He'd put something on the wall or adapted something. He'd made new windows. Or a new fence or a new door. Or bricked up a door again. He'd have made a new pool for the garden. Or they hosted a big barbeque, where he'd put up a tent to cover his grill. And so on.

This shaped the idea of "building something." Actually, a lot of neighbors and people in my hometown just "built stuff." It was a normal process. Often, there was no big planning process. They just "built stuff."

Later in my life I moved to Vienna and studied architecture. I learned a lot about theory, history, the design process, and the evolution of architecture. It often seemed intensely complicated and hard. You need to have a lot of knowledge and play by the rules. I got the distinct feeling that "building something" is actually very complex and difficult.

I mostly forgot about my childhood memories and those first impressions of building architecture as something intuitive and improvised. But, after some years and several visits back home, I started noticing again how much of my hometown was built by neighbors and anonymous people. I noticed the quality and beauty of those buildings, the lightness in the process, and the difference in their makeshift approach.

I started to take a lot of pictures, trying to capture all the details. For example, thinking about material and approach: maybe you use three different types of bricks because it's what you already have at home. Or take the execution of common architectural elements such as walls, windows, doors, and gutters. They differ in form and shape. The patina. The function and use of the building or structure often plays a certain role, but the design seems pretty intuitive.

I found a lot of simple structures that were of great interest. They were built with great skill and accuracy. Piles of useful materials were organized in a beautiful manner.

I try to look at these places from different angles. To reduce and enlarge the scale. To zoom in and out. To pay attention to small details. To sharpen the focus through abstraction. It has become a part of my everyday praxis. My routine.

Even when I'm on holiday I am guided by those places. I visited the seaside in the north of France. I discovered some beach houses that you can rent for the day. Every house looked almost identical. I took some pictures of the site. I thought of my neighbor friend. I thought about people just "building something." I thought about "the house with the blue roof."

Photography:
Nikola Hergovich, from his photo series *Naive Architektur*, 2023

Colors in Contemporary Urban Praxis

Francesco Caneschi

Colors are a fundamental tool for the contemporary transformation of public space within our cities. Both in regenerating abandoned plots and transforming pointlessly large streets, colors help us in the fight against two tremendous present-day ideologies: the apologetic Modernist use of white, which becomes gray with time, and the ideology of private motorized transportation, namely the car.

The use of color in these interventions can create immediate changes, in projects that would otherwise require years.

This essay will briefly describe what contemporary urban praxis is and how color is linked to this gentle urban revolution.

It begins with Aldo van Eyck in post-war Amsterdam, moving through to the Spanish recession at the beginning of the twenty-first century, presenting currently existing examples alongside those that are still being designed today. In doing so, this text demonstrates how colors can fight old urban concepts and stimulate contemporary debate about how our cities should be.

We do not live in a black and white world. In fact, our built environment is full of colors, but usually not the bright ones. In most cities, colors are used to highlight something, as in their use on road signs. Bright colors generally highlight crucial information or dangers, making you pay attention to something. After road signs, advertising devices are the most colorful elements in built environments across the Global North. Elements that need to "pop up," to "hook" you in, or alert you to something.

Urban Praxis

In contemporary urban praxis,[1,2] colors become a tool to show that something is changing. But what's urban praxis? It's the discipline that situates itself at the crossroads of public space, urbanism, architecture, and design.

Many possible names are given to this crossroads: tactical urbanism,[3,4] urban acupuncture,[5] place-making,[6] incremental urbanism. The term urban praxis was chosen for the title of this essay, but incremental urbanism would also fit here.

The problem with tactical urbanism is that the term is now mainstream, meaning that many people use it without a proper awareness of what it means. Though tactical urbanism is now widely accepted by a large audience, it stands without doubt for an attitude toward urban transformation that's nonetheless highly innovative. One of the main characteristics of this approach is the use of temporary[7] experiments, operating with a small budget.

Because of the scarcity of color in built environments, and because paints are a more affordable tool for transforming a space than many others, color has become one of the prominent tools for urban praxis.

Modernism's White

White with a capital W has been a tool, too. At the outset of Modernism, when professionals sought solutions that could be adopted everywhere in the world, white was a tool that allowed for the easy

Fig. 1
"Zeedijk Playground,"
Aldo van Eyck, Amsterdam

application of a common approach. It was the color—even if it's not technically a color—that could unify the global effort toward a "better" and "modern" built environment. The grid and the color white have been twin tools for Modernist urbanism.

The flaws of the Modern movement have already been extensively analyzed,[8,9,10,11,12] and nowadays numerous publications and architectural practices have adopted the use of color in their projects as a trademark.

Obviously, color has many historical references within the urban environment, from the example of Greek temples through to the town of Sarzana in Italy.

One of the problems with Modernism's white was that, in reality, the white of the drawings became the gray of the concrete. The grayness of this utopian solemnity was, at the same time, both the cause and result of an increasing gulf between those who designed urban environments and the people who inhabited them.

"Zeedijk Playground" by Aldo van Eyck

Since the beginning of the twentieth century—though with only a few examples spanning the period between the end of the Second World War and the nineties—many case studies have subverted this distance from citizens through the use of color.

One of the first examples of the use of color in urban regeneration—one that we could define as incremental urbanism—was Amsterdam's Zeedijk playground, designed by Aldo van Eyck.[13]

Fig. 2
"Esto no es un Solar," Arquitectos Grávalos Di Monte, Saragoza, Grávalos Di Monte

The walls surrounding this previously abandoned plot were painted as part of the project by artist Joost van Roojen, van Eyck's brother-in-law. The artist painted the surrounding walls with geometric abstractions, using rectangles and a few circular shapes. Though the colors he used were visually sympathetic to their surroundings, at the same time they stood out as brighter. What looks like a choice probably emerged out of sheer contingency, given that this was the first experiment of its kind. The formal approach of van Eyck's playground was thus reflected in the chromatic choices of van Roojen's paintings and vice versa. The design process for van Eyck's playgrounds began with the design of flooring based on an asymmetrical matrix of polygons. He would then break the rigidity of the flooring's straight lines with curved shapes. These shapes could be climbing structures, sand pits, or other sculptural elements.

In this example, the colors and layout were integrated into the urban environment while standing out from the surrounding area.

"Esto no es un Solar" by Grávalos Di Monte

This approach evolved in "Esto no es un Solar"[14] in Zaragoza in 2006. This project had the same spatial focus of van Eyck's playgrounds, except using abandoned plots rather than land destroyed by the war. "Esto no es un Solar" means "this is not an abandoned plot."

During the Spanish recession, the municipality asked the architects Grávalos Di Monte to develop a program that could employ as many people as possible

Fig. 3
"Luchtsingel," ZUS, Rotterdam,
Ossip van Duivenbode

with jobs that required low building technology. The architects decided to regenerate small urban plots with minimal interventions, thus painting was again a perfect tool. In this example, which is relatively recent in chronological terms, colors were used in a more extravagant way but with the same design approach: a geometric matrix deformed by curved shapes. The aims of the projects realized under this program were pretty similar to the aims of the Dutch project: namely, transforming an abandoned place into a lively one on a shoestring budget, using playgrounds.

The “Luchtsingel” bridge by ZUS

Colors can change the viewer’s perception at many different scales. The Luchtsingel bridge and passageway in Rotterdam, a project developed by ZUS [Zones Urbaines Sensibles], is a great example of the use of color in a temporary infrastructure.

> “Decades after their separation, the 400-meter-long Luchtsingel pedestrian bridge has reconnected three districts in the heart of Rotterdam. The Luchtsingel is the world’s first piece of public infrastructure to be accomplished through crowdfunding. Together with the new public spaces, including the Delftsehof, Dakakker, Pompenburg Park, and the Hofplein Station Roof Park, a “three-dimensional cityscape” has arisen. Based on the idea of Permanent Temporality, the Luchtsingel introduces a new way of

Fig. 4
Piazze Aperte, AMAT, Milano,
Comune di Milano

> making a city. This means using the city's evolutionary character and existing forms as a starting point."[15]

In this particular case, color was used both because it was a conceptual choice at the start of the design process and because of the construction detail used to pave the bridge: the yellow planks. These planks were crowdfunded and engraved with the names of the donors. When I visited it, walking across the bridge was visually powerful: the yellow contrasted steeply with the gray of the surrounding infrastructures, differentiating this infrastructure from those surrounding it.

Being very narrow, the only way to see the yellow color is by being inside the bridge or looking at it from an aerial viewpoint. If you want to design something that stands out from its environment, the use of bright color is fundamental. Color here is both a mode of design and a form of communication.

"Milano Piazze Aperte"

"Milano Piazze Aperte" is a project developed by the municipality of Milan, together with AMAT,[16] Bloomberg Associates, NACTO,[17] and GDCI.[18]

Piazze Aperte means "Open Squares," and the aim of these initiatives is to create incremental experiments in the urban environment. Progressively, though instigating temporary events, underused streets and parking lots are transformed into new configurations.

Fig. 5
"Prossima Apertura," Orizzontale,
Aprilia, Alessandro Imbriaco

After the Second World War, the ideology of street design privileged the use of the car as opposed to other means of transportation, a simplified choice that resulted in making roads as large as possible. One effect of this was the erosion of the basic, everyday encounters fostered by more ecological modes of transportation that preceded the rise of cars: namely, bicycles and pedestrians.

This project, reminiscent of the previous ones presented in this essay, deployed color to transform gray spaces of asphalt and concrete into vibrant squares.

In the initial phase of the program, the colors used were ones administrations already had in abundance: the paints used for the horizontal layout of street signs.

"Prossima Apertura" by Orizzontale

"Prossima Apertura"[19] Aprilia is one of the first incremental urbanism designs in Italy. All phases of the design have been developed across different disciplines and various levels of interaction.

This project was led by Orizzontale,[20] a collective focused on public spaces. They often use colors to highlight the concepts of their design or pick out some particular detail.

This urban regeneration project involved color in the design process from its very beginning: in advertising the project, during the participative process, and in the final design of the square.

Color was initially used to advertise that something new was happening: the project's first act was

Fig. 6
"Frame," ECÒL, Milano, Prato Centenaro,
Agnese Morganti, Comune di Milano

to install a big billboard in the "abandoned" plot, which was a vacant shop instead of a public space. It featured yellow stripes alongside the title of the project, "Opening Soon."

The participative process included the performance *Paint'nPlay*, by the artist Rub Kandy. Participants were invited to design geometric shapes on the ground and walls, indicating a path through the space using anamorphic designs.

Toward the end of the project, this yellow was also used in the open-air gym and playground.

The yellow and gray used in the project were also chosen as Pantone's colors of 2021,[21] the year in which the design was completed.

"Frame" by ECÒL

The fortieth square realized in the Piazze Aperte Program was Prato Centenaro, the outcome of a design competition won by ECÒL.[22] The concept of their proposal was to use the crosswalk as a decorative element, extending and transforming the familiar white stripes to create a more playful landscape. The badly redesigned crossroad became a square through the simple use of white paint, populated by new urban furniture. "Frame," the project's title, seems to refer to the pattern of the design as well as the project's function: to host new scenes of public life. This example helps us avoid falling into a new ideology, where color is a necessary tool for urban regeneration. Color, or in this case white paint, is a tool that can be used to engage a space and the community living around it.

Obviously, design here is as important as color. In this case, a series of concentric squares create a two-fold result: they pinpoint the benches and the ping pong table while at the same time creating a geometric pattern that can be freely interpreted by passers-by.

Findings

The case studies presented here involve colors, or paint, as one of their main visual elements. All of the projects cited in this essay were located in the Global North, more specifically in Europe, where the Modernist urban matrix has characterized almost every aspect of the environment. It appears that color is one tool through which we can "edit" the grayness of the Global North's urban environment.

Another characteristic linking the examples presented in this text is their impermanence—many of these projects, at least in the initial phases, are temporary. Often, one of the problems with color is the supposed risk of getting bored. However, if the intervention is temporary, any colors that don't work well can be altered in the future.

The temporariness of colors in contemporary urban praxis is opposed to the so-called "permanence" of Modernism's enduring white. Color also favors the collaboration between artist and architect, leveling the design process by bringing it closer to the people instead of confining it to the "professional" disciplines. Colors are often linked to play and, as a result, to playgrounds. In fact, colors transform the urban landscape into a playscape, overriding the rigid codes and ideologies under which public space is “normally” produced.

Notes

1 Jochen Becker et al., eds., *Glossary of Urban Praxis: Towards a Manifesto* (Berlin: GbK, 2020): https://www.urbanepraxis.berlin/wp-content/uploads/2021/11/UP_Glossar_en.pdf.
2 Markus Bader and Rosario Talevi, eds., *Exploration in urban practice* (Barcelona: dpr-barcelona, 2017).
3 Mike Lydon and Anthony Garcia, *Tactical Urbanism: Short-term action for long-term change* (Washington: Island Press, 2015).
4 Francesco Caneschi, *Tactical Urbanism and DIY Architecture: for a gentle urban revolution* (Chișinău: Lambert Academic Publishing, 2021).
5 Jamie Lerner, *Urban Acupuncture* (Washington: Island Press, 2014).
6 Cara Courage et al., eds., *The Routledge Handbook of Placemaking* (London: Routledge, 2020).
7 Peter Bishop and Lesley Williams, *The Temporary City* (London and New York: Routledge, 2012).
8 Peter Blake, *Form Follows Fiasco* (Boston: Atlantic, 1974).
9 Robert Venturi, *Complexity and Contradiction in Architecture* (New York: The Museum of Modern Art, 1966).
10 Brent C. Brolin, *The Failure of Modern Architecture* (London: Cassel and Collier MacMillan Publisher, 1976).
11 Craig Buckley and Jean-Louis Violeau, eds., *Utopie: Texts and Projects, 1967–1978* (Los Angeles: Semiotexte, 2011).
12 Douglas Murphy, *The Architecture of Failure* (Alresford: Zero Books, 2012).
13 Liane Lefaivre, *Aldo van Eyck: the Playgrounds and the City* (Rotterdam: NAI Publisher, 2002).
14 "Esto-no-es-un-solar," accessed December 1, 2022, https://paisajetransversal.org/2012/06/esto-no-es-un-solar-i-el-proyecto/.
15 Kristian Koreman and Elma van Boxel, *Cities of Permanent Temporality* (Rotterdam: Nai 010 Publisher, 2019).
16 "Agenzia Mobilità Ambiente e Territorio," accessed December 1, 2022, https://www.amat-mi.it/.
17 "National Association of City Transportation Officials," accessed December 1, 2022, https://nacto.org/.
18 "Global Designing Cities Initiative," accessed December 1, 2022, https://globaldesigningcities.org/2022/05/24/piazze_aperte_report-en/.

19 “Prossima Apertura,” accessed December 1, 2022, https://prossimaapertura.orizzontale.org/en/.
20 “Orizzontale,” accessed December 1, 2022, http://www.orizzontale.org/en/.
21 “Pantone’s color of the year,” accessed December 1, 2022, https://www.pantone.com/articles/past-colors-of-the-year/color-of-the-year-2021.
22 “ECÒL,” accessed December 1, 2022, https://ecol.studio/.

#kommwir-streichen

Home Colors: from Sahara Yellow to Sand Breeze

Jan Engelke

The color scheme of the living space is the residents' business. Architects rarely play a role in the selection of colors. Far more important are color trends set by, for example, home magazines. Those seeking to understand how color developed in everyday living since the post-war period will find no useful source material in the established, renowned media of the architectural discipline. Better to flip through the colorful pages of *Schöner Wohnen.*

The magazine *Schöner Wohnen – Journal für Haus, Wohnung, Garten und Gastlichkeit* was launched in 1960 as a branch of *Constanze*, Germany's most successful women's magazine at the time.[1] The genes of this magazine shaped the accessible, entertaining, and often emotional character of *Schöner Wohnen.* With a reach of over 3,000,000 readers, it soon became the most popular interior design magazine in the German-speaking world. The magazine presented a colorful mix of living tips, home stories, and gardening topics alongside lavish advertising columns from the so-called *Wirtschaftswunder* (economic miracle) years. Some of the editors had studied under Egon Eiermann in Karlsruhe during the 1950s, and worked on sharing actual architectural insights. Understanding architectural representations was just as relevant as constructive and architectural-historical knowledge. *Schöner Wohnen* can therefore be considered a popular architecture magazine. The use of color within one's own four walls was one of its most important topics.

One's own apartment can be painted any way you desire. But what about a rented apartment?

Leases usually require that the apartment be painted in "bright, neutral, opaque colors" upon moving out. Exactly what shade of color is meant by this is an excellent matter of debate—even in court. In legal terms, it is assumed "that colorful designs such as (delicate) lime green or light blue may be 'bright,' but do not match many types of furnishings and therefore cannot be considered 'neutral'... ." A "bright green kitchen," "blue-painted door frames or color-painted radiators," "color-painted natural wood frames," or a "painting with 'red full tone'" were all the subjects of lawsuits, deemed unacceptable at the time of handover. However, while living there, tenants have the right to choose the decoration and color of the apartment themselves. In the context of so-called "cosmetic repairs," which also include painting and wallpapering, there may be no contractual specifications that "restrict the design of personal living space."[2]

The Home is often described as a private matter and its design is seen as an expression of something deeply "personal." The home becomes part of a self-narrative: Salvatore Pisani describes the design of one's own home as "me-architecture," as a "lived vita and alter ego,"[3] while for Pierre Bourdieu, one's own four walls are a "material good that, like clothing, but in perpetuity, becomes perceptible to all."[4] Given such gravity, it becomes impossible to decide on the "right" color for a living space.

Here, *Schöner Wohnen* (Fig. 1) jumped to the rescue: in the 1960s it offered a "complete color design with material samples, manufacturer and price information" (SW 1970/01, p. 9) without anyone even

Fig. 1
Cozy colors: *Schöner Wohnen* color scale in "soft and gentle tones"

coming to the apartment. The color consultation was to be done by letter with photos sent by post. Interior design advice for the price of a magazine—the beauty of the idea lies in the democratization of professional design for people who couldn't afford the cost of an individual design. However, it appears that it was not only readers who were interested.

Since the end of the 1960s, *Schöner Wohnen* has published a "SW color scale" every year, according to which it defined "guiding colors" with titles like "Sahara," "Colorado," or "Toscana." During this time, the editorial team's color trends reached millions of readers every month, many of whom decorated their homes according to the new color scale. As the increasing commercialization of living during the so-called "economic miracle" led to an avalanche of colorful products flooding living spaces, trade and industry sensed big business in high-frequency emerging trends. They began to match products, textiles, and furniture to this color palette—all in the hope that people would, from that moment on, refurnish their homes every year if the old sofa no longer matched the new "guiding color." Paint manufacturers advertised that they could mix paints to match the new scale (SW 01/1971, p. 23), a clinker brick factory produced glazed façade tiles in the "Sahara" shade (SW 06/1973, p. 182), and aluminum windows were even offered in the same shade (SW 10/1970, p. 64). Matching curtains could also be ordered (SW 10/1972, p. 354); indeed, by the end of the 1970s, Mercedes Benz had painted the popular W123 model in both "Colorado Beige" and "Sahara Yellow" (Fig. 2).

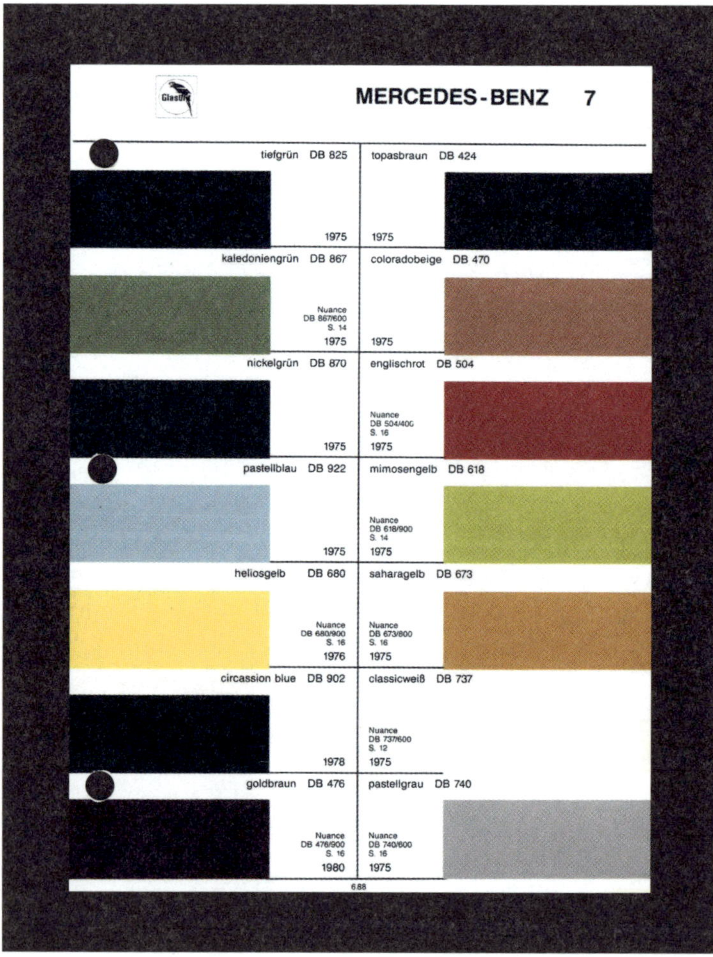

Fig. 2
Workshop color specification
Mercedes Benz

In the editorial of the first issue, the editors stated: "We do not wish to impose a particular style on you, our esteemed readers. On the contrary—we would like to tell you: don't live and reside schematically, but personally." (SW 01/1960, p. 3) However, it remains dubious how "personal" the color design of living spaces can truly be when living trends largely determine the choice of colors. Irene Nierhaus considers the individualization of the home conveyed here to be a "basic feature of the mythification of living in the modern age." This is accompanied by a certain "empowerment of the residents." In connection with the "desire to live" fomented by home magazines, however, "in this context, the better and more beautiful serves to fuel the desire and at the same time its normalization."[5]

Just as ambiguous were the trends themselves, as a closer look at the underlying concepts reveals: the SW color scheme "Tuscany" could only superficially serve the wanderlust of a generation—without the luxury of EasyJet—in which travel was still gradually becoming affordable for a majority. These were also clichés of the concept of the "South," wherein the desire for a relaxed, simple, beautiful lifestyle, was painted onto the walls. This becomes apparent, for example, when the title "Color orgies à la hippie" in a home story refers to "exotic hippie eye candy." The accompanying picture illustrates this notion of "exotic" with plenty of plants and a window into a second, turquoise-blue interior (Fig. 3). "'Sahara', the new interior color" is contrasted with "monotony": "[t]he desert is alive, full of color," states the editorial introducing

Fig. 3
Turquoise-blue colors and houseplants
as “exotic hippie eye candy”

the new collection (SW 09/1969, p. 5). Why are beige living room walls and cars imbued with a connection to the Sahara when sandy Sylt is in fact much closer to home? Infused with exoticizing and neo-colonial imagery, a touch of "adventure" was domesticated in the choice of wallpaper. Simultaneously, new television sets broadcast the first cooking programs in which Clemens Wilmenrod[6] invented a recipe named "Arabisches Reiterfleisch," or inextricably linked the term "Hawaii" (in many West German memories) with a boiled ham and cheese toast garnished with a slice of pineapple.[7]

Binary gender relations were also linked to color concepts in *Schöner Wohnen*. In the early 1970s, *Schöner Wohnen* presented readers with a puzzle titled "Test your talent for living." The prize question was: "Which furniture ... would you use to furnish a romantic, graceful and playful, feminine and charming room?" A bedroom with a dressing table was to be designed; the furnishings were characterized by "very restrained colors" and "soft color transitions" (SW 06/1971, pp. 80–81). In the next issue, the "masculine-objective, functional" (SW 07/1971, p. 58) study was the focus. Here, "clear lines, sharply angled shapes ... and few colors" are requested. Many rooms in *Schöner Wohnen* are stereotypically gendered in terms of color.[8]

Schöner Wohnen increasingly intensified its co-operation with the industry: at the end of the 1960s, *Schöner Wohnen* advertised a collaboration with the Kaufhof department store, which sold furnishings in colors that matched the trend colors (SW 09/1968,

p. 181) and launched its own wallpaper collection in collaboration with wallpaper manufacturers (SW 11/1969, p. 8). By the early 1970s, major paint manufacturers such as Caperol already had the *Schöner Wohnen* color palette in their product range (SW 04/ 1973, p. 79). When publishing and print media began to decline in the 1990s and *Schöner Wohnen* faced financial difficulties, the magazine not only produced new "color trends," but also—in cooperation with the manufacturer Brillux—made matching paint available in every DIY store under the *Schöner Wohnen* label. According to editorial circles, the commercialization of these paint colors—through regularly instigating new, and self-determined trends—was the magazine's economic salvation.

Today, remote color consultation is still provided via their Instagram account: over 45,000 accounts are supplied with the hottest color trends by @schönerwohnenfarbe and can share pictures of their own freshly painted walls under the hashtag #kommwirstreichen ("Come on, let's paint!"), which can also be seen as an invitation. The pictures that get the most likes are those that look just like the studio shots of @schönerwohnenfarbe. In line with the current boom in the terms "sustainable" and "regional," "Natural chalk paint" is now trending, with the shades "Coastal Mist," "Spring Awakening," "Forest Whispers," "Brook Ripples," and "Sand Breeze" being sold by large hardware store chains. The 2.5-liter bucket costs €39.95.

Notes

1 By the early 1970s, circulation had quickly risen to around 450,000 copies with foreign supplements in eight languages. As a popular waiting room read, *Schöner Wohnen* reached over 5,000,000 "heads of household" in the early 1970s and became the most successful interior design magazine in West Germany.

2 Judgment of the German Federal Court of Justice dated June 18, 2008, file number BGH VIII ZR 224/07.

3 Salvatore Pisani, "Ich-Architektur. Das Haus als gelebte Vita und Alter Ego," *Ein Haus wie ich: die gebaute Autobiographie in der Moderne*, ed. Salvatore Pisani, Elisabeth Oy-Marra and Katharina Siebenmorgen (Bielefeld: Transcript, 2014), 9–39.

4 Pierre Bourdieu, Salah Bouhedja, Rosine Christin, Claire Givry, "Un placement de père de famille," *Actes de la recherche en sciences sociales*, vol. 81–82 (1990): 6–33.

5 Irene Nierhaus, "Seiten des Wohnens – Wohnzeitschriften und ihr medialer und gesellschaftspolitischer Display," *FKW Zeitschrift für Geschlechterforschung und visuelle Kultur* 64, no.1: 18–28 (here: . 18, 20).

6 The actor Carl Clemens Hahn (1906–1967) was the first German television chef in the 1950s and 1960s, appearing in the program "Clemens Wilmenrod bittet zu Tisch" (NWDR) under his stage name.

7 The pineapple was first introduced to Hawaii on colonial plantations and its production history has little to do with the "exotic" notions of its West German connoisseurs. For the colonial history of the Dole Hawaiian Pineapple Company, see Garry Y. Okihiro, *Pineapple culture: a history of the tropical and temperate zones* (Berkeley: University of California Press, 2010).

8 For detailed analysis of this material, see Rosanna Umbach, "Un/Gewohnte Beziehungsweisen: Visuelle Politiken des Familialen im *Schöner Wohnen* Magazin der 1960er und 1970er Jahre," (PhD diss., University of Bremen 2022), 116.

Max Otto Zitzelsberger in Conversation

With Michael Hafner and Katharina Hohenwarter

Fig. 1
Suggested color combination for a poster
by Max Otto Zitzelsberger

This conversation evolved from an e-mail correspondence in which an attempt was made to discuss the colors for a poster announcing a guest lecture by Max Otto Zitzelsberger at the Graz University of Technology.

27.10.2023, 11:19

MOZ Between Enie van de Meiklokjes and *Schlumpfeis*[1], I simply feel comfortable!

MH/KH The fact you feel comfortable working with color is repeatedly evident in your work. However, such a sense of comfort is not especially common in our discipline. Even if the use of color, after a temporary abstinence—probably a reflex of postmodernity—seems to be playing an increasing role again in recent architectural production. Where do you think this discomfort comes from?

MOZ There is probably something to this diagnosis: the "temporary abstinence(s)" of color is "probably a reflex of postmodernity." I'll go further. With reference to Germany, much worse can be predicted ... . It's not only color that has been lost, but also form. It seems to me that these two phenomena must be considered together as regards architecture in Germany: architecture here is dominated by conservative values. It is "neat" and "rational," it"blends in," "fulfills its purpose," and above all "doesn't hurt anyone." This "architecture" does not offend. Color is always an expression of emotion and passion. It makes the "German soul" nervous. The land of "poets and thinkers" is above all one of "calculation" and "concern" ;-)

I'm getting to the point, as you can see. In my years as an "architect," this "rational" complacency became increasingly unappealing to me. Every work is a critique of another work. In this sense, we can also express ourselves with architecture. I like another variation of this sentence even better: the unbuilt is the criticism of the built. Or, to put it another way, colorfulness is a criticism of colorlessness.

MH/KH From your critical assessment, it appears that you attribute a similar significance to color and form, that you view them as mutually dependent and as symptoms of the problems you mentioned. But isn't it also the case that—especially in the flat, shallow, media-effective production of architecture—color has proven to be a suitable tool for disguising the loss of form?

We also ask ourselves to whom exactly your (very understandable) criticism is addressed? The direction of the attributes you mention is not always that obvious to us. Who is the bearer of these conservative values and who is pandering to whom? "To blend in," "to fulfill its purpose," "neatness," and "rationality" are phrases that are already inherent in architectural training and are elevated to quality criteria.

To what extent is your built work perhaps also a critique of your own architectural biography?

MOZ Now I think we're getting a little deeper into the matter!

I agree with your claim that color is an easy way to effectively conceal the loss of form. Perhaps that's why my interest in color has waned somewhat recently, in favor of form.

Now to the question of who my criticism of "loss" is directed at. It is primarily the architects themselves: on the one hand, the self-employed who put their goods on the market of the "decent ones." On the other hand, the associations and institutions that align their building policy precisely with the aforementioned "values" and define the formal language of the "conformist" as "building culture." Furthermore, it is the clients, both private and public, who demand this thoroughly uninspired "architecture" and discredit everything else as "formalism."

This mélange of actors also defines the insipid and majority-compatible competition results as the lowest common denominator. Technical and organizational issues also dominate third party-funded research. Research on design and expression that is "architectural" in the true sense of the word is generally not recognized academically. You mentioned teaching yourself.

During my studies at the Technical University of Munich, the topics of "appropriateness," "blending in," and "fulfillment of purpose" were definitely present. In this respect, my built and—above all—my unbuilt work is also a critique of my own architectural and social biography, respectively; namely the conservative "values" that I absorbed and internalized with my mother's milk in a "bourgeois" parental home.

Fig. 2
Pavilion eaves side by
Max Otto Zitzelsberger

MH/KH Seeking responsibility within your own profession is very honorable.

"We would, if we were allowed to," is a popular proclamation among architects. But we ask ourselves—and this brings us back to color—how much more would we do if we could? As already discussed, color—along with form—is an essential serving tool of architectural design. For a long time, we have trained ourselves to make our architecture measurable in Excel sheets, wherein architectural "form," "expression," and, above all, quality are difficult to depict. To what extent do you share our suspicion that we have lost our expertise in dealing with tools such as color—to put it economically, that we have "outsourced" it from architecture?

MOZ "Would we still, if wc were allowed to?" I don't have a concrete answer to this question. A society defines its culture and culture, in turn, has an influence on its society. The "built" is part of culture and, as such, an expression of society. Let's think back to the time after the Reformation, when the Catholic South was forced to redefine itself. Architecture and art functioned as tools of this social transformation process. The concept of space in the Baroque differs fundamentally from that of the Renaissance. Michelangelo made his own contribution to this. Did he help shape the new social ideals through his architectural innovations or were they the result of these sociological changes?

There is no clear answer to this question. The two are interdependent. Societies are never static.

Fig. 3
Pavilion gable side by
Max Otto Zitzelsberger

They are constantly changing. Sometimes more slowly, sometimes faster. This is yet another phenomenon. Societies are never homogeneous, even if it may seem so in retrospect. There can be very different—even controversial—ideas and views within such a "society," which in turn establish their own cultural ideas.

For centuries, architecture has been an expression of sovereign power. Architecture as the result of a democratic negotiation process is still a very recent phenomenon and is in the process of being replaced by autocratic tendencies. Understanding space as an expression of certain values, such as human rights or tolerance, should be a concern for all of us. And I don't mean that pathetically at all, but very seriously. Our profession is still too fond of private spaces, places of retreat, cocoons. But we should devote our interest to the space of the community, the places that we are allowed to help shape. This space is in the process of being eroded.

My generation has grown up under the illusion that it can be taken for granted. But we are currently being made aware that this space of community must be constantly redefined and renegotiated. To what extent form and color should play a role here remains to be discussed. In any case, neither phenomenon can simply be an end in itself.

MH/KH However, if one tries to follow your initial diagnosis in this context—now somewhat polemically shortened, of course—of an architectural profession that "fulfills its purpose" in "rational accordance" with clients, with its architecture whose form "neatly" tries to take a certain image of society into account; then one would like to grant architecture a more active role—if architecture can achieve this. More than just being a mere reflection of a certain *zeitgeist*. Thus, purely hypothetically, one would attribute significance to every means of expression, including color, and detach it from being merely an end in itself. What purpose, or end, does color pursue in your work? At the beginning, you spoke of an architecture that doesn't hurt anyone. Does architecture have to hurt? Does color have to hurt? Your use of color, albeit progressive, is far too beautiful for that.

MOZ Exactly. As you say: "One would like to grant architecture a more active role ... . More than just being a mere reflection of a certain *zeitgeist*. So, hypothetically, one would attribute meaning to every means of expression, including color, and detach it from being an end in itself." But how? So far, I haven't come up with anything better than only realizing those projects I feel like doing and trying to make a difference within them, for example through color. But what use is architecture that nobody wants?

We are currently pursuing a completely different strategy in the office. We are trying to turn the tables, in the sense of an "inverse" method, whereby we think of the projects in a radically clear, distinct, and unpretentious way. We use abstract colors like white, for example. Though perhaps white is not a color? Or perhaps the material itself determines the color.

MH/KH To prevent the word "color" from becoming an end in itself—and because you should always stop when you have an idea about how to proceed—we want to finish our conversation with these prospects. We will be eagerly following which forms and colors your new strategies will lead you to, and how you will deal with the brightest of all colors and its nuances. Thank you, Max!

Notes

1 "Schlumpfeis" is a name for blue vanilla-flavored ice cream, which is particularly popular with children. The term refers to the skin color of the comic characters "The Smurfs" ("Die Schlümpfe" in German).

RGB Trauma

HPO
Giorgio Scanelli and Riccardo Simioni

Fig. 1

Our collective consciousness as a working entity emerged when we first felt the need to communicate our work, both internally and externally, using the fastest medium available: our smartphones.

According to Lacan, human subjectivity emerges from the mirror image that the child recognizes as an image of himself, aided by the presence of an Other who mediates this acknowledgement through speech and language. Just as the subject is born from an image mediated by language, so too our consciousness as a working collective was born from the preverbal use of images—through which it necessarily emerged and is forever captured. Our collective *forma mentis* was shaped while using the WhatsApp image editor to create sketches on smartphones (Fig. 1), as a way to quickly share design drafts between a large group of people: rcsulting in a huge ensemble of photos with childlike fingertip drawings in pure RGB dyes (255,0,0), (0,255,0), and (0,0,255).

Tools have always determined artistic production and diffusion, and we are interested in how default settings can affect both thinking and designing. Decisions made by programmers on the other side of the world place strict rules on the designing process: AutoCAD, Revit, Rhino, Photoshop, Illustrator, Instagram, and WhatsApp, are all the result of some code lines. The simpler the input, the more interesting it becomes to play with it. In our case, WhatsApp became a shared space in which ideas took shape, and in its simplicity its photo editor represents a fundamental tool in our process.

As well, R, G, and B served as a crucial means of sharing the project outcomes with other people: an identity took form as soon as we appeared on social media, diving into the big game and big lie of architectural content on Instagram. As students posting little ephemeral works and WIPs, the RGB Default Æsthetic served as a statement to outline an identity: the pure RGB look, loud and almost dramatic, became a tool for breaking out of the infinite flatness of social media content. Furthermore, picking the most immediate hues on the color-wheel is a direct consequence of the denial of overthinking and overworking, which are diffused symptoms of inefficient human labor organization in architectural practices.

Shortly thereafter, with the onset of the pandemic, an even larger number of individuals migrated to digital screens. During this time, the boundaries between the physical and digital worlds became increasingly permeable, with content constantly flowing between the two. In our view, pure RGB colours represented one of the many potential keys to navigate and cross these boundaries. As these colours can be visualised only by electronic output sources, their physical manifestation is limited to devices like projectors or displays. However, RGB-like hues can also be imitated through special inks and textiles, as seen in green screens used for the Chroma Key compositing. Generation Y was among the first to be captivated by behind-the-scenes footage from films like *The Matrix* and *The Lord of the Rings*, where actors were shown performing against pure green backdrops, which were later replaced with CGI environments.

The use of a quasi-RGB green, not normally present in other objects in the scene, ensures that only the background is cropped and replaced in the post-production. While working with the Chroma Key visual effect in an exhibition setup in Berlin, we aimed to recreate a digital model space within a physical museum pavilion, seeking materials that closely matched RGB green (Fig. 2). This effect was ultimately achieved using a fluorescent pigment.

Despite the aforementioned physical apparitions, RGB colors "remain in light"—deeply rooted in electronic visualization, they are used to display the entire palette through additive mixing whether static or dynamic. Different frameworks were invented for photographic devices and CRT displays to create colored dynamic images through the additive synthesis of the three main colors (Fig. 3). This performative quality of electronically displayed colours was notably explored by Daniel J. Sandin, who was among the first to experiment with video synthesisers. Between 1969 and 1973, Sandin developed the Sandin Image Processor, a device often described as the "video equivalent of a Moog audio synthesizer." The processor accepted basic video signals and manipulated them in a manner akin to how a Moog synth modifies audio signals.

The translation of sounds and colors into electronic signals began with the creation of elemental signs such as waveforms (sine, triangle, saw, and pulse) and RGB (255,0,0), (0,255,0), and (0,0,255)—each of which, perceived by the senses in the pure form, is almost annoying. The mixing of these basic inputs,

Fig. 2

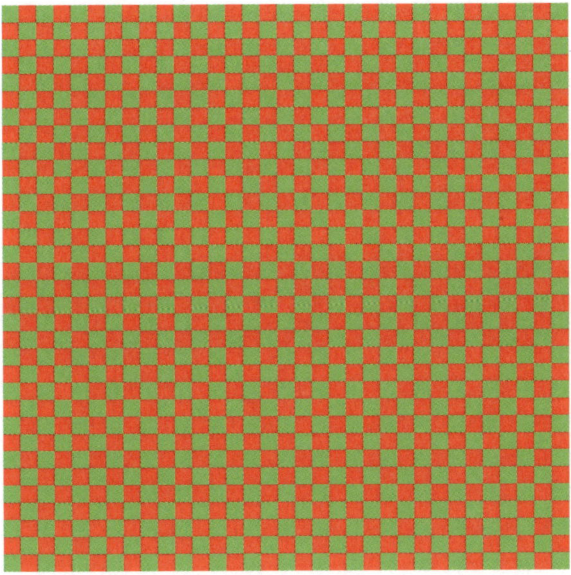

Fig. 3

however, results in digital reproductions that are more similar to "real" sounds and colors and therefore sensorially pleasant. RGB represents the most banal default starting point from which to pursue unexpectedly high tension in visuals. The traumatic limit of this tension between basic colors is represented by the harmfulness of colored flashing lights in digital displays and their consequences related to epilepsy. In pop culture, this phenomenon became quite famous in 1997, when a *Pokémon* episode containing flashing lights was aired on TV Tokyo, causing multiple epileptic seizures in about 700 young spectators. During some scenes, almost full-screen red and blue flashes were alternated at a rate of 12 Hz for six seconds. After the event, the network set specific technical rules regarding frequency and timing in animated colors displayed on TV screens, and concern about visual effects in electronic animations and video games grew. This episode shows how, in its migration from natural to electronic, color gained additional cultural and sensorial properties and opened itself to more fields of influence, acquiring the capacity to represent a primitive design starting point and a primary source of design tension. This virtuous tension is at its most intense when the simplest primary inputs are combined in the least elaborate way—creating according to this principle of simplicity enables a more streamlined structure of thought through which further artistic and architectural aspects of the project can develop.

evltube, "5 Minute Romp thru the IP," YouTube video, 3:52, December 13, 2007, https://www.youtube.comwatch?v=8qh6jRzjmcY/.

Jacques Lacan, *Le séminaire de Jacques Lacan: Le moi dans la théorie de Freud et dans la technique de la psychanalyse*, ed. by Jacques-Alain Miller (Paris: Le Seuil, 1973).

Gordon Fung, "audiovisual performance on Sandin Image Processor (11/8/23)," YouTube video, 32:30, December 11, 2023, https://www.youtube.com/watch?v=fn2aKYnIKyQ/.

"Sandin Image Processor," Electronic Visualization Laboratory of University of Illinois Chicago website, accessed October 10, 2024, https://www.evl.uic.edu/research/1934.

Takeo Takahashi and Yasuo Tsukahara, "Pocket Monster incident and low luminance visual stimuli, in Pediatrics International," *Blackwell Science Asia* 40, no. 6 (1998): 631–637.

Sheryl Wudunn, "TV Cartoon's Flashes Send 700 Japanese Into Seizures," *The New York Times*, December 18, 1997.

Coating Absolute

Alexander Barina

The text is intended as a plea for monochrome paint as the *ultima ratio* of urban planning practice. The logic of monochromaticity is outlined on the basis of various examples from the field of fashion (such as the Roman Catholic dress code) and the visual arts (monochrome series by Nancy Rubins and Daniel Firman) and examined with regard to its applicability on a building and urban scale. This culminates in a proclamation of monochrome embalming, which can be understood here as a method of "further building" in the sense of a final urban sacrifice (and is thus diametrically opposed to an absolutist Haussmannian building regulation).

The linking of colors with feelings, temperatures, and states of emotion has already been widely and sufficiently discussed in the past, in a variety of circular diagrams. It seems absurd to me to associate red with anything other than warmth and arousal unless—and this brings us to the linking on a semiotic level—I am thinking of the red-socked ankle cuffs of the political left and the papal cardinals, who could not be more different in spirit, but are said to look confusingly similar from big toe to calf, which indicates that the interpretative sovereignty of colors also requires social negotiations.[1]

So it comes as no surprise that if one wanted to buy scarlet socks—not just any shade of red, but colorfast after washing, hanging brightly and richly on the washing line, like a display tied around the ankle shining in eternal (255,36,0)—the Via S. Chiara in Rome is the predestined clerical address for this venture. On offer at Gammarelli, the Pope's tailor,[2] are various clerical costumes and seasonal hangings. The range available to secular male customers is limited to socks in a very restricted color palette, namely black, purple, and red. As with every fashion trend, the Catholic Church demonstrates a healthy tendency toward uniformity that promotes group affiliation and, incidentally, consumer behavior—black socks are reserved for priests, the color purple for bishops, and red for cardinals—which makes it possible, should the rest of the work "uniform" not already convey this from every seam and every buttonhole to read the corresponding professional denomination from glimpsing the ankles while kneeling with bowed head: Mr. Cardinal, or to finally build a bridge to an architectural discussion: I am a cardinal.

The uniform, especially if it is made of the finest fabrics but in a monochrome color, offers a welcome opportunity to conceal inadequacies of a physical nature as well as character weaknesses of any kind under the garment—to distract from or diffuse them among the crowd of monochrome uniform wearers. In this sense, color is a fairly simple and economical (albeit sometimes devious) trick through which to simulate a sense of affiliation, even if every sock conceals the same bare skin. So why not establish a connection to architecture, to the building material, when even [Gottfried] Semper referred to the material character of color? There are those buildings it is worth diverting attention from and those buildings one would like to see *de facto* merge with their surroundings as the *ultima ratio*—these exist city up, city down. A skin-tight monochrome coating could be applied to both existing and new buildings in order to combine a heterogeneous multitude into a figurative unity, blending into an existing hue.

That there does not necessarily have to be an obvious or compelling connection between color, or the application of color and an entity, can be clearly comprehended in the sculptures of Daniel Firman and Nancy Rubins. Each artist creates sculptures in different color editions, both in polychrome and monochrome. In contrast to Firman, who produces the sculptures in his "Gathering" series from different objects, Rubins used the same object, a canoe, to construct her project *Big Edge*, the repetition merging the vessels into one new form. Comparing these with *Monochrome I* and *II*, the steel *epigones* of *Big Edge*, the two differ significantly in their relationship to the perception of overall figure and individual object, and thus also in their relationship to perceived scale—which is not unimportant given their sheer physical size. The distinctive coloring of the industrially manufactured canoes makes it easier to read the individual boats as discrete entities within a colorful whole—providing they are not also painted polychrome. The monochrome steel adaptation, on the other hand, shifts the focus away from the readymade to a holistic and volumetric perception, an effect that can only occur when the colored boats are seen at a great distance—namely, when the individual boats are no longer recognizable as such (despite their different colors) and everything blurs into chromatic noise. The monochrome color scheme thus creates a state of limbo: it is simultaneously legible in the overall figure and in the individual object, viewed at close range from the sculpture. As in Daniel Firman's work, it becomes irrelevant whether it is composed of the same element or a montage of different elements. Both variants demand the complete comprehension of their artistic intention by a moving observer.

Streets and buildings consist of repetitive as well as unique elements and components that are legible in their façades, whether in their proportions, materials, or color scheme. Multiple buildings can also repeat themselves or be soloists when they form an urban figure, while this urban unit can in turn appear in a multiplicity or singularity and continue to integrate itself into an even larger overall context. We imagine an arbitrary section of the city that, after lengthy discussion or perhaps through aggressive entrepreneurship, has been classified politically and structurally as unworthy of preservation. It is in an artificial "coma" during this process, consecrated for demolition but not yet demolished. How old, and in what condition the building actually is, is irrelevant. Our buildings would be located in a red-beige-gray-sand-colored district, and we would choose exactly this color to paint the houses, from the base to the ridge. We apply the brush in the knowledge that it is irrelevant for the monochrome paint whether elements are repeated or not. Applied from top to bottom, the paint would gradually cover all surfaces and edges, roofs, roof tiles and gutters, window frames, reveals, sills and casements, running into all cracks and coating all signs of ageing and use in a sea of color;

no corner would be omitted. Porches, railings, and entrance doors, every doorbell button and letterbox slot—everything would be painted. The paint would seep into all levels of the exterior wall below, so that under every cover strip and every sheet of metal, even on the bright wooden surfaces untouched by sunlight, a layer of paint would be applied. After drying, one could only uncover more and more new red-beige-gray-sand-colored layers by scratching. Under each layer of paint there would be another layer of paint and so on. The description of a house as red-beige-gray-sand-colored would never be more accurate. The façade would be permeated by paint as if by formaldehyde and the decaying process would behalted; the painter's scaffolding would become a *catafalque*.

But where would we draw the line, marking the boundary with the original state, and how would we do this? Where does the red sock end? Does it only cover the ankle, or the whole calf? How does it relate to the whole leg? Does it peek out from under the garment? Or does it merge with it, perhaps tucked into a red shoe?

Whether freestanding or integrated into a structure, the exterior could be painted entirely, up to and including the transition to the ground. Or a well-considered edge could be drawn across the façade from top to bottom, as the figurative character of the coherent color surface would ultimately be more important than the complete envelopment. Color and figure would not have to be limited to the building but could spill over into the areas directly in front of, next to, and behind it, additionally forcing the sense of a structure that interlocks with its surroundings. Much like to Yves Klein's *Relief éponge bleu*, this would emphasize surface qualities over material differences. Ultimately, it was not about the actual disappearance of a building whose physical presence and corporeality were fully preserved. It would not be a conversion or renovation, as nothing would be structurally changed or even technically improved. At best, it would be an embalming, a final deep coat of paint marking the transition from the conversion cycle to urban planning nirvana, rebirth excluded. A monochrome coat of paint that is not limited to individual elements and surfaces but is absolute.

Notes

1 Goethe's classification of the color red in his color wheel study (which is located in the area between reason and fantasy) does not flatter either of the two red camps.

2 Founded by Giovanni Antonio Gammarelli in 1798, the tailor's shop specialized in dressing the clergy of Rome. It was under Pope Pius XI (1922–1932) that the company was finally made the Pope's tailor.

Contributions #–2

Contributions	Dominant Color
31/44 Architects	
ANAH	
architecture uncomfortable workshop	
ARHIV architecture & urbanism	
Atelier Amont	
ATELIERDACOSTA	
Atelier do Corvo	
Atelier Starzak Strebicki	
Atelier van Berlo	
BATIMENTS	
BELT	
Bovenbouw Architectuur	
Bruncken Frett Architekten	
BUERO41A	
BUREAU	
CABINET	
CHYBIK + KRISTOF	
Cierto Estudio	
coabitare	
COCI	
COMTE/MEUWLY	
Corpo Atelier	
CORREIA/RAGAZZI ARQUITECTOS	
Čović + Köroğlu	
Demo Working Group	
Detour Universe	
draftworks* architects	
Eagles of Architecture	
EBBA	
Enrique Espinosa (Eeestudio) / Lys Villalba	

EHRL BIELICKY
fabulism
fala
False Mirror Office
David Fink, Lukas Fink, Tobias Fink
Franziska Singer Architektur
GANG Atelier
GIPP arkitektur
Groothuijse de Boer architecten
GROSZSTADT
Habsburg Isele Architekten
Heide & von Beckerath
Hobiger Feichtner Architekt*Innen
HOH Architecten
Howland Evans Architects
HPO
IMS Studio
Institut für- gegen Baukultur
Ivo Poças Martins
Johansen Skovsted Arkitekter
JOUD VERGELY BEAUDOIN ARCHITECTES
KAWAHARA KRAUSE ARCHITECTS
Keßler Plescher Architekten
Klemen Breitfuss Architekt ETH
KOGAA
KOSMOS
Leeser Architecture
MacIver-Ek Chevroulet
Mair-Paar Büro für Architektur
Max Otto Zitzelsberger – Architekt BDA

Meier Unger

Michael Maltzan Architecture

Michael Reindel

MONADNOCK

MRND

Multerer Architekten

Muoto

Noreile Breen

NOWADAYS office

Nuno Melo Sousa

Office Kim Lenschow

pablo saiz del rio + vivian rotie

Point Supreme Architects

Present Forms

PROFFERLO Architecture

Sarah Naira

Sauter von Moos

Schaub Zwicky Architekt:innen

SCHNEIDER TÜRTSCHER

SET Architects

Studio Andreas Lechner

studio eder krenn

Studio Eidola

Studio Jakob Sellaoui

STUDIOLO

studiospazio

SUJETS OBJETS /

Theo De Meyer

Wallimann Reichen

Wilhelm Scheruebl – TAB collective

31/44 Architects

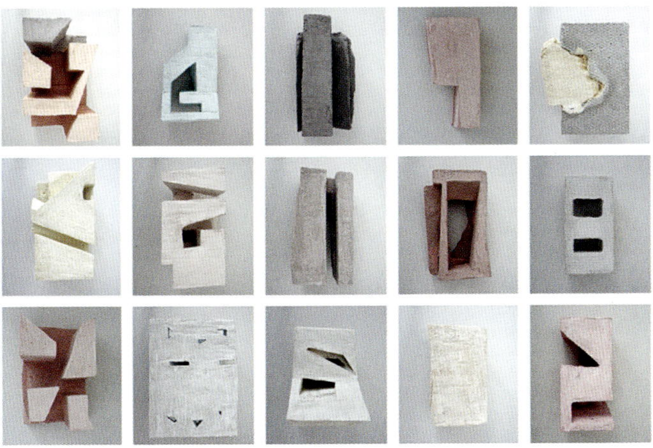

ANAH

architecture uncomfortable workshop

ARHIV architecture & urbanism

Atelier Amont

ATELIERDACOSTA

Atelier do Corvo

Atelier Starzak Strebicki

Atelier van Berlo

BATIMENTS

BELT

Bovenbouw Architectuur

Bruncken Frett Architekten

BUERO41A

BUREAU

CABINET

CHYBIK + KRISTOF

Cierto Estudio

coabitare

COCI

COMTE/MEUWLY

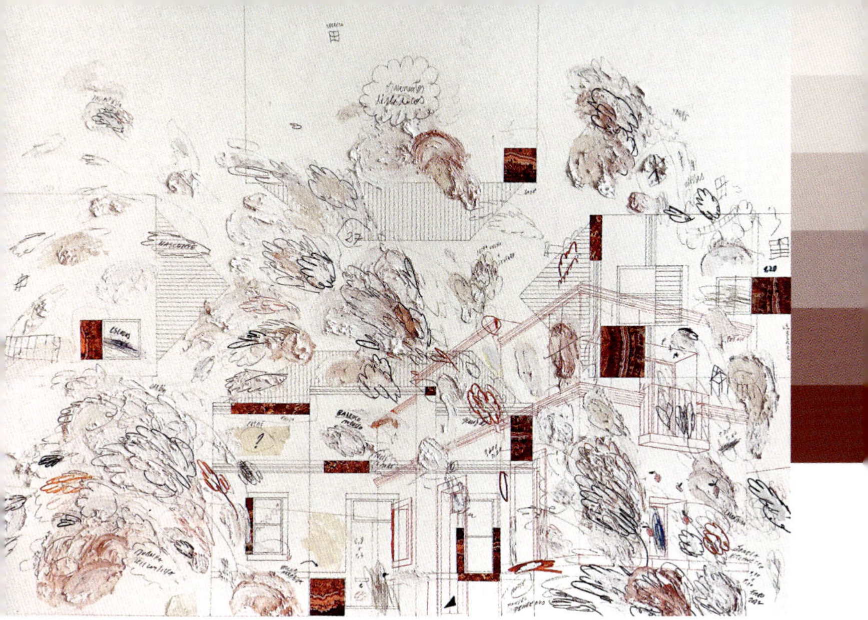

Corpo Atelier

CORREIA/RAGAZZI ARQUITECTOS

Čović + Köroğlu

Demo Working Group

Detour Universe

draftworks* architects

Eagles of Architecture

EBBA

Enrique Espinosa (Eeestudio) / Lys Villalba

EHRL BIELICKY

fabulism

fala

False Mirror Office

David Fink, Lukas Fink, Tobias Fink

Franziska Singer Architektur

GANG Atelier

GIPP arkitektur

Groothuijse de Boer architecten

GROSZSTADT

Habsburg Isele Architekten

Heide & von Beckerath

Hobiger Feichtner Architekt*innen

HOH Architecten

Howland Evans Architects

HPO

IMS Studio

Daktylothek Institut für- gegen Baukultur

Erde Argentinierstraße 39

Hummus

Lavagranulat

Wohnbaurot

Marmorsplitt

Kiefernrindenmulch

Blähton

Glitter

Moos dunkel

Rot

Schimmel

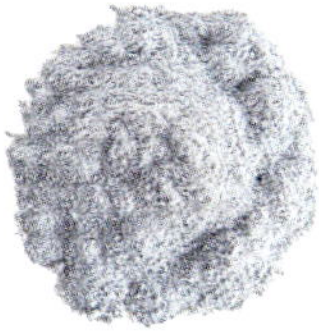
Fast weiß

Atelier schwarz

Moos hell

Mulch grün hell

Leim

Institut für- gegen Baukultur

Ivo Poças Martins

Johansen Skovsted Arkitekter

JOUD VERGELY BEAUDOIN ARCHITECTES

KAWAHARA KRAUSE ARCHITECTS

Keßler Plescher Architekten

Klemen Breitfuss Architekt ETH

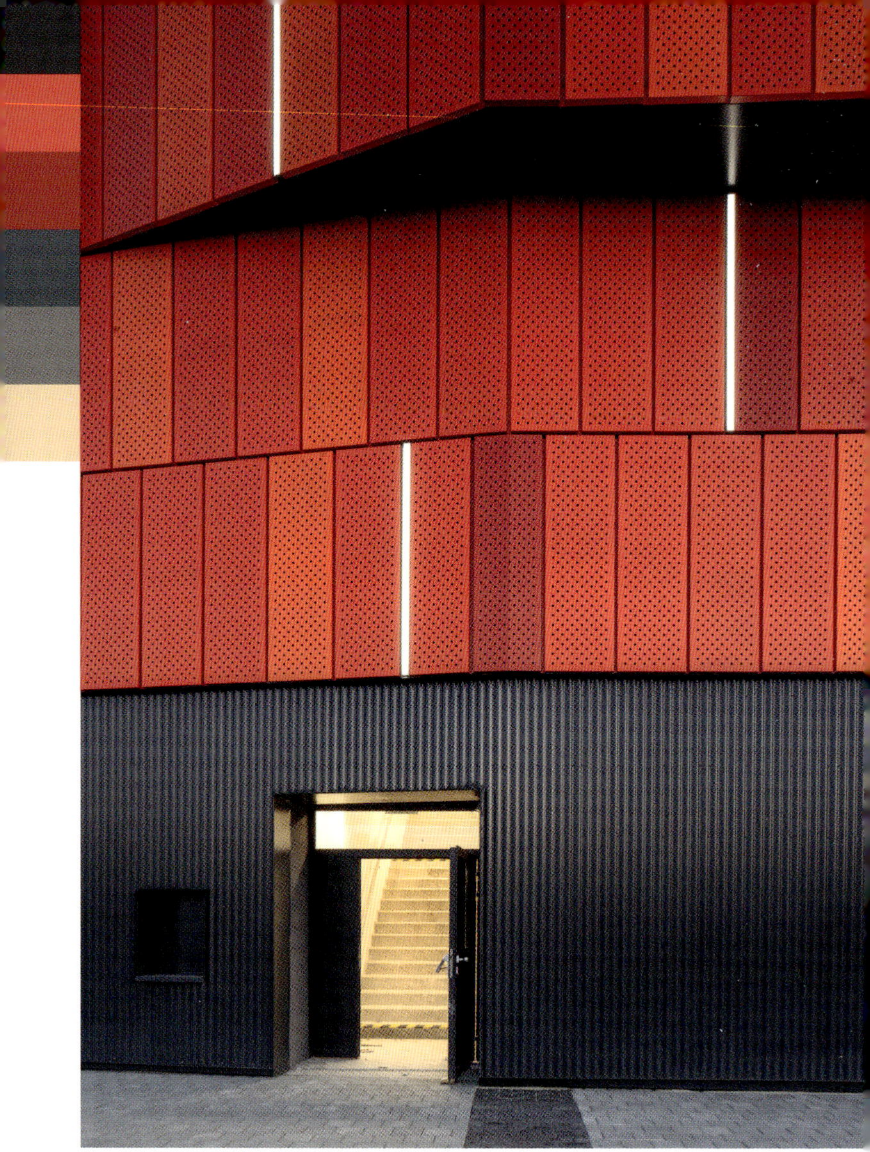

KOGAA

KOSMOS

Leeser Architecture

MacIver-Ek Chevroulet

Mair-Paar Büro für Architektur

Max Otto Zitzelsberger – Architekt BDA

Meier Unger

Michael Maltzan Architecture

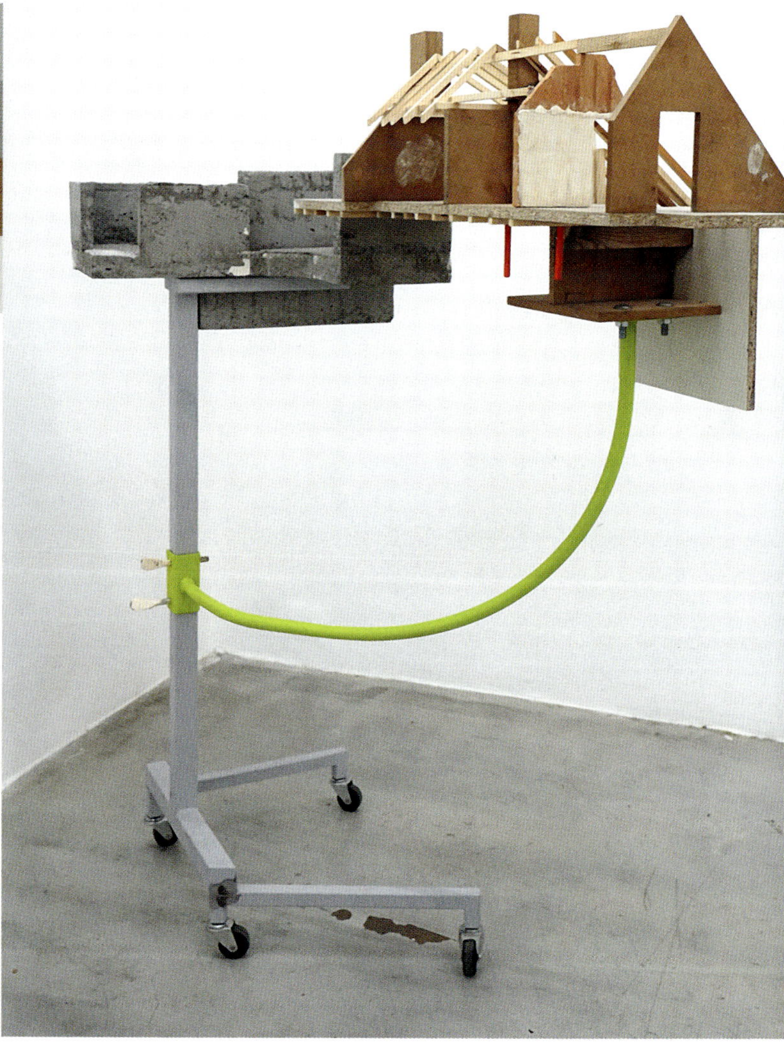

Michael Reindel

MONADNOCK

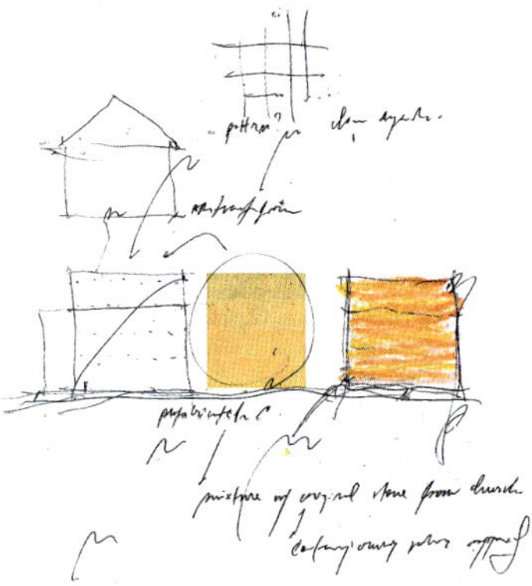

Multerer Architekten

Muoto

Noreile Breen

NOWADAYS office

Nuno Melo Sousa

Office Kim Lenschow

pablo saiz del rio + vivian rotie

Point Supreme Architects

Present Forms

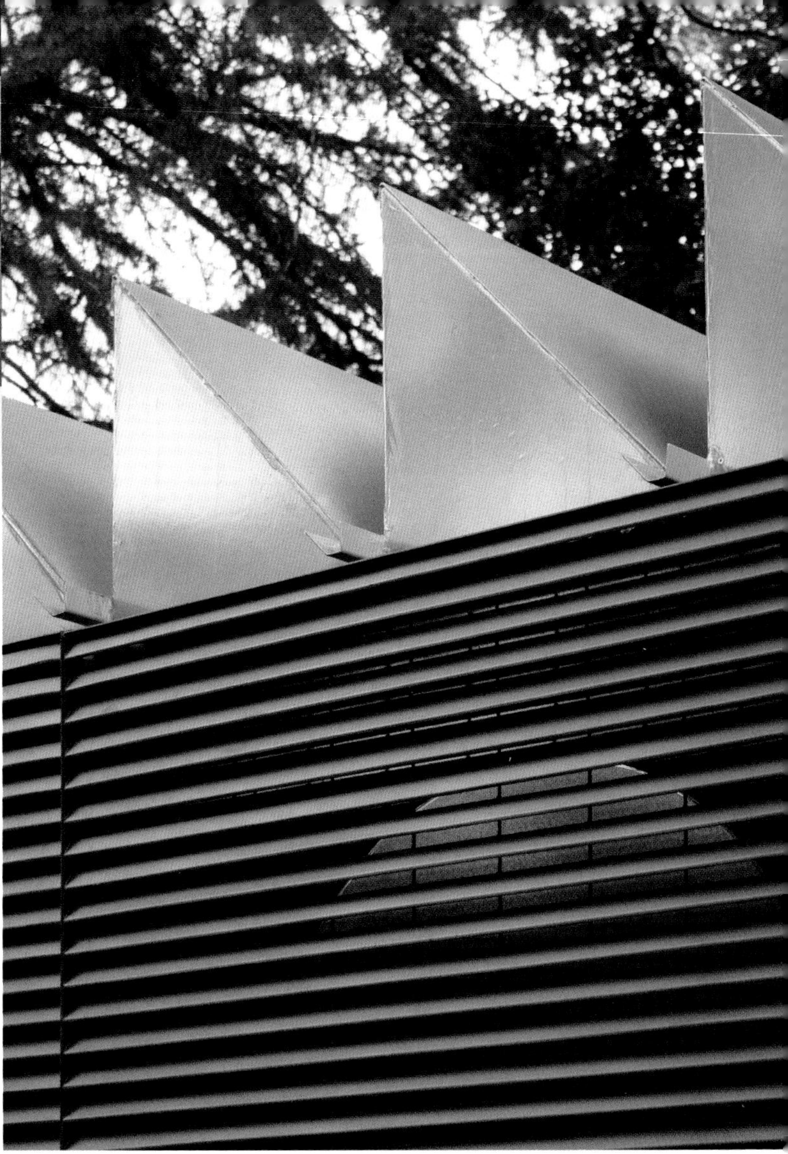

PROFFERLO Architecture

Sarah Naira

Sauter von Moos

Schaub Zwicky Architekt:innen

SCHNEIDER TÜRTSCHER

SET Architects

Studio Andreas Lechner

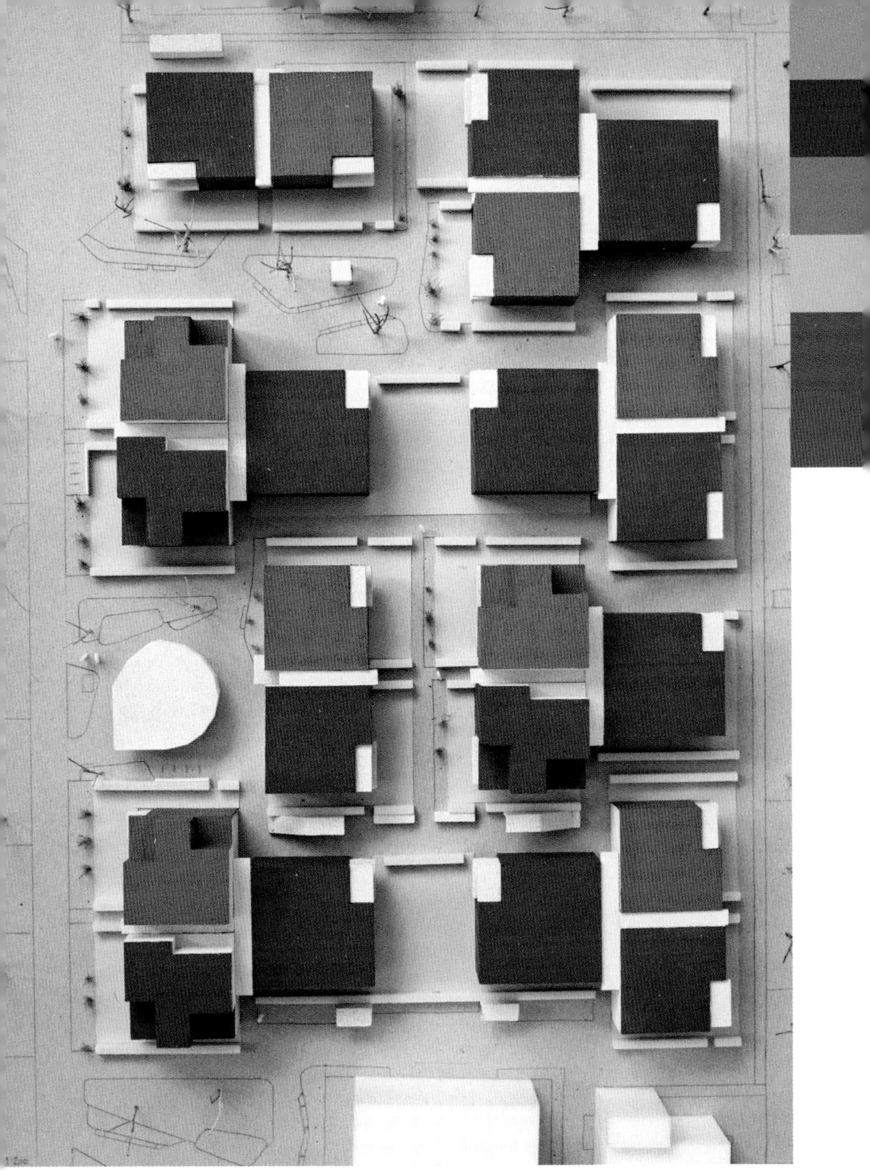

studio eder krenn

Studio Eidola

Studio Jakob Sellaoui

STUDIOLO

studiospazio

SUJETS OBJETS/

Theo De Meyer

Wallimann Reichen

Wilhelm Scheruebl – TAB collective

The Dizzying Universe of Karl Gerstner and Vilém Flusser

Franziska Hederer

Review of the Article by Karl Gerstner: "Vilém Flusser and the colors" in *Kunstforum International*

> "Color is light, i.e., the visible spectrum of electromagnetic waves; it has to do with physics. Color is substance, i.e., matter with which we can represent it; it therefore has to do with chemistry. Color is perception, i.e., the process that takes place in our eyes; it therefore has to do with physiology. Color is sensation, i.e., what our brain makes of perception; it therefore has to do with psychology.
>
> There is another science involved in color: mathematics, which deals with color as a structural problem. It classifies the variety of colors according to objective parameters. And designs models in which each individual color tone has its precisely defined place."[1]

This is how Karl Gerstner opens his 1986 book *Die Formen der Farben – Über die Wechselwirkung der visuellen Elemente* [The Forms of Color: The Interaction of Visual Elements]. The book is based on Gerstner's statement: "Form is the body of color—color is the soul of form."

This could also be the subject of what Gerstner describes as a "synergetic encounter"[2] with Vilém Flusser, in which they aimed to develop a new color code, bringing colors into a rational system. Together, they established a denotative system with the precision of the numerical code, in which each color is assigned a neutral basic meaning in the sense of a symbolic value. Although this endeavor still remained unfinished even after Flusser's death in 1991—and perhaps may never have been completed at all—Gerstner considers the fragments of the process worthy of recording.

The endeavor to bring colors into a rational system has existed since ancient times, as Gerstner makes clear in his book. However, this amounted to no more than rudimentary, metaphysical speculation. Differentiated models only emerged with the beginning of the exact natural sciences in the seventeenth century. And it was not until the beginning of the nineteenth century that Philipp Otto Runge, a German Romantic painter, created the first coherent and descriptive model:

> "It has the shape of a sphere that can be read like a globe. White stands for the North Pole, black for the South Pole and the color wheel for the equator: the pure colors from yellow via red, blue and green back to yellow. The poles are connected by lines of longitude across the equator and intersected by lines of latitude. In this way, fields are created on the surface of the sphere, which are filled with intermediate colors."[3]

"Aren't there already color codes in abundance?" asks Gerstner in view of the numerous color models that have been created since Runge. "In heraldry? In road traffic? In psychology? In signaling ethics? In everyday life?"[4] For Gerstner, it is clear that Flusser

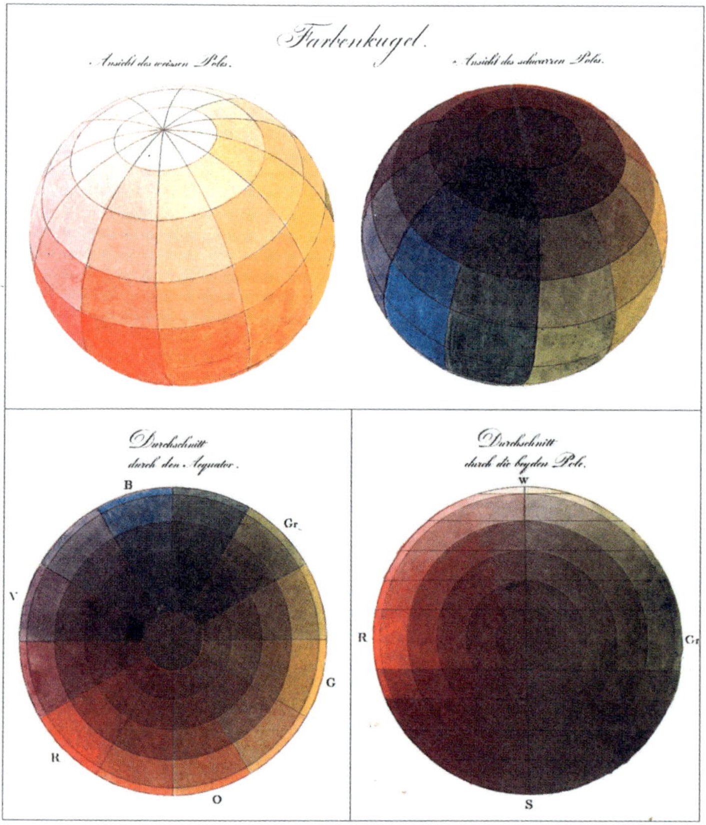

Fig. 1
Philipp Otto Runge's color sphere "or construction of the relationship of all compounds to each other, and in their complete affinity."

did not mean these color codes, which are too imprecise and ambiguous.

Vilém Flusser, who was concerned with the decline of written culture throughout his life, had the idea of replacing the obsolete alphabet as the code for language, instead expanding numbers as the code for logic and postulating a new cultural stage by developing a color code analogous to numbers. By aligning the color code and the number code, thinking was to be made accessible to the senses and vice versa. As Flusser remarks: "The symbols of the numerical codes signify quantities. Whoever says 'quantify' means: break down into rations. He means the gesture of rational thinking. The colors, when used as symbols, signify qualities. And if you say 'qualify,' you mean 'make tangible.'"[3] Color is then understood in the totality of colors as a structure in which each color belongs to a precisely defined place in a multidimensional system, presented as an ordered universe. Such a color code would also be a tool for bridging the divide between scientific and artistic thinking.

Flusser saw the color code as a beacon of hope for aesthetic thinking. Rationality should be aestheticized and aesthetics, in the sense of imagination, should be subjected to the rational.

Flusser suggests that throughout previous cultural periods, in which objects were transcoded into images, images into texts, and texts into numbers, our knowledge became increasingly distanced from experience, from what the sensory organs convey. Numbers form the basis of the modern world, its science and technology. For Flusser and Gerstner, the question arises as to how our culture would have developed if not only numbers, but also colors and forms had influenced our paradigms, and if scientific thought was brought into phenomenological alignment with aesthetic experience.

The special attraction of the color universe is its finite nature on the one hand, and its unlimited divisibility—or "miscibility," as Gerstner terms it—on the other. While the universe of numbers is infinite from zero in the direction of plus and minus, the universe of colors extends infinitely inwards, starting from the outer limits of black and white, light and dark. While numbers have ten primary signs (or digits), the color universe is defined by the spectral colors of light, or by Maxwell's three primary colors, plus black and white. Gerstner describes the model of the color universe conceived by him and Flusser, which he calls *Colorarium*,[5] in the form of a crystal lattice which is to be "played" like an instrument. Comprised by intersecting nodes, colors are generated electronically as light at the point of contact.

In an architectural sense, Flusser and Gerstner's theory could be understood in terms of construction's relation to numbers and composition's relation to color. One could call this the separation (or even non-separation) of core form and art form, as Karl Bötticher put it in the organic context of his work on tectonics. Bötticher dealt with the closer definition of the relationship between the interior and exterior of buildings.

The aim would be to distinguish the material component from the symbolic component or to bring them closer together. In analogy to Flusser and

Gerstner's idea of the color code, the art form would then also be assigned a neutral basic meaning in the sense of symbolism and not connotative, i.e., subjective, emotional, or associative. Art and core form would complement one another.

The dizzying aspect would probably lie in the simultaneity of absolution and the infinity of symbolic forms. Gerstner describes this as an interplay of "procedural processes from all areas of science, business and technology."[6] Whether such an endeavor can be successful without incurring too much mental gymnastics remains an open question for now. Perhaps this goal is too ambitious. The collaboration between Gerstner and Flusser did not come to a concrete conclusion, since they apparently had bigger plans—namely, the creation of "a monument like the 'Géode' in Paris, with an audience in the midst of the colors"... .[7]

Notes

1 Karl Gerstner, *Die Formen der Farben* (Frankfurt: Verlag Athenäum, 1986), 13.

2 Karl Gerstner, "Vilém Flusser und die Farben," *Kunstforum International*, 117 (1992), accessed December 25, 2022, https://www.kunstforum.de/artikel/vilem-flusser-und-die-farben/.

3 Gerstner, *The Forms of Color*, 14.

4 Gerstner, *Kunstforum*.

5 Ibid.

6 Ibid.

7 Ibid.

Le Rouge et le Noir in Löwenbräu Blue

The Colorful Rooms of Ferdinando Scarfiotti

Julian Müller

Fig. 1
Red Room, *American Gigolo*, 1980,
Director: Paul Schrader

"Color me your color, baby / Color me your car / Color me your color, darling / I know who you are." With these lines, sung by Debbie Harry, and a tracking shot following a black Mercedes 450SL, the film begins. Its director, Paul Schrader, became known for writing a screenplay about a lost *Taxi Driver* on a lonely, paranoid mission through New York City. In this film, however, we migrate from the East to the West Coast. The setting is not dreary New York, but sunny Los Angeles.

After the black Mercedes has been parked, we see the driver trying on a jacket in an imposing boutique. Apart from floor-to-ceiling mirrors, this boutique is decorated in bright red—red walls, red seating, red carpet. In the very next shot, we discover that the driver is obviously not just a lover of red boutiques and black cars. He says goodbye to an elderly woman at her front door, a little too intimate for a normal friendship, but nevertheless professional. Thus, this film (made in the year 1980) already in its first two minutes plays as cleverly as it does casually with moral standards and cultural references. In minute three, we learn what the driver is called: his name is Julian. This name is by no means a coincidence, but an allusion to perhaps the most famous Julien in literary history, as will become clear further in the course of the film. Its symbolism will fully come into view when we drive past a nightclub that is named, of all things, "Sorel."

And just as the provincial upstart Julien Sorel, the main character in Stendhal's *Le Rouge et le Noir* (1830), moves through nineteenth century French

Fig. 2
Black Room, *American Gigolo*, 1980,
Director: Paul Schrader

society—between the military (red) and the clergy (black), between the revolution (red) and the restoration (black), between love (red) and death (black)—so too Julian Kaye, the main character in *American Gigolo*, is permanently moving through strikingly colored spaces—through red boutiques, black nightclubs, red bars. These rooms are essential protagonists in this film. It is hard to ignore them and especially their colors. The Italian art director and production designer Ferdinando Scarfiotti, who also designed films such as *The Conformist, Scarface*, and *Toys*, was responsible for these rooms.

Schrader calls him his "mentor and master." "He gave me eyes," Schrader recently said in an interview with Sofia Coppola.[1] Alongside the encounter with Charles Eames, the meeting with Scarfiotti was groundbreaking not only for the set design of Schrader's films, but above all for the way he conceived of his films from then on: he no longer viewed them just from the perspective of plot, but as a visual piece of work. Scarfiotti taught Schrader—who, as he himself repeatedly emphasizes, grew up in the sparse, white rooms of Protestant churches where nothing but the word counted—the importance of images and colors.

Nowhere else can this be seen as clearly as in Schrader and Scarfiotti's first collaboration, the marvelous color film *American Gigolo* (1980). For architects, this film is a document that can hardly be overestimated since it is both a film about colors and about rooms. These colorful rooms are by no means merely backgrounds or scenery, they are essential carriers of the action. The protagonist, Julian Kaye—who is not

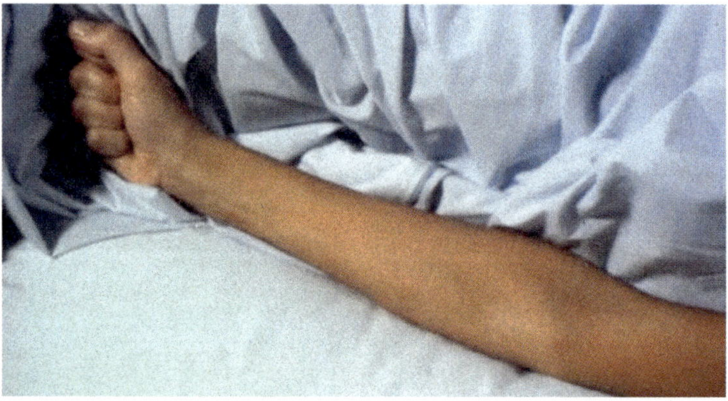

Fig. 3
Löwenbräu Blue, *American Gigolo*, 1980,
Director: Paul Schrader

a hero or an actor in the strict sense of the word—no longer "performs" any actions in these colored spaces, but rather becomes a mere element of action, someone who simply "drifts around [while] things happen to [him]."[2] Our usual idea of space and action is thus reversed. The colors are used less allegorically than atmospherically. They sometimes tell us more about the state and inner life of the protagonist than his actual actions.

Something else must be mentioned here: Schrader's initial idea was not to make a film about a professional gigolo, but rather a film about Los Angeles in general. For Schrader, however, it was clear from the beginning that he did not want to approach this city as a local. Instead, he took the path of maximum distancing: "I wanted to de-losangelize Los Angeles."[3] He achieved this by being less interested in the city's self-image than in its image to others. For this he enlisted the help of three foreigners, or to be more precise, three Italians. Giorgio Armani—then only little-known internationally—was responsible for the costumes, Giorgio Moroder contributed the terrific soundtrack, and Ferdinando Scarfiotti was, as already mentioned, the art director.

These diversions—via Italy and a specifically Italian-Catholic view of Los Angeles—allowed Schrader to capture the atmosphere, the sound and, above all, the colors of the city. Not so much the real city of Los Angeles, however, but rather the city of Los Angeles as a space of imagination and fascination. Besides the shots of iconic places like Rodeo Drive, the Pacific Coast Highway in Malibu, or the Beverly

Fig. 4
Case of Löwenbräu Beer, *Scarface*, 1983,
Director: Brian De Palma

Hills Hotel, it is the colorful rooms that shape the image of this dream city. These rooms are mostly red and black. But sometimes they are also bright blue.

This blue, which perfectly matches the Californian light, has its origins (funnily enough) not in California, but in Bavaria. Ferdinando Scarfiotti, who, like Giorgio Moroder, spent a period of his life in Munich, is said to have loved the blue of a very specific Munich brewery,[4] which, incidentally, he repeatedly incorporated into his films. And so, it is *Löwenbräu Blue* that in the end defines this colorful film, this Italian-Bavarian imagination of Los Angeles. Despite all the red and black, it is remembered as perhaps the dominant color of *American Gigolo*, not least because the only "real" love scenes in the film are steeped in this blue.

Notes

1 See "This is How it Should End with Paul Schrader and Sofia Coppola," A24, May 30, 2018, https://a24films.com/notes/2018/05/episode-04-this-is-how-it-should-end-with-paul-schrader-sofia-coppola.
2 Interview with Paul Schrader, in *California über alles* (Vol. 2), eds. Georg Diez and Christopher Roth (Zürich: Edition Patrick Frey, 2010), 46.
3 See "This is How it Should End."
4 Interview with Paul Schrader, 39.

How Do Colors Get Into the City?

Walking and Understanding Vienna's Urban Color Space

wohnlabor
Rebekka Hirschberg and Anna Jäger

> "Looking—we often don't do that anymore. Urban planning, traffic planning, sociology—aren't they just studied from behind a desk? Strollology seeks out places and their life and tries to rediscover the act of observation. Observing means opening up new perspectives, trying out new ways of seeing, perceiving the unfamiliar, uncovering disturbing elements, making mistakes and becoming aware of oneself … . Strollology wants to gain a different understanding of time and space. Strollers are already slower through the use of their feet—and since they walk because they want to, and not in order to arrive somewhere, they are unpredictable in time. Strollology sees space as a construct of perception—in that sense, as ambiguous."[1] Lucius Burckhardt

About two and a half years ago, we started exploring urban space on foot in order to gain a "different understanding" of it—inspired by Lucius Burckhardt. These walks and critical reflections gave rise to the Stadtstücke platform, a walking experiment based on the perception of urban space.[2] The interactive platform collects *Stadtstücke* (city pieces)—snapshots and comments on places—and everyone is invited to take part. The aim is to understand the city as a place of democratic negotiation that affects us all and to examine the appropriation of public space.

Some of our walks through the city are dedicated to a specific theme—such as vacancy, planting, inner courtyards of municipal buildings, borders, or, as in this case, colors. For this text, we took two walks: through the historic and the new, through the center and periphery of Vienna, focusing our attention on colors in particular. On our walks, we often ask ourselves why things are the way they are and what decisions have led to this. The design conditions and the framework behind things usually remain invisible to people in urban spaces.

The question that we asked ourselves during the walk added another layer to the text. This second layer deals with ideas, laws, planning principles, and other negotiation processes that have contributed to the characteristics of urban space or continue to do so.

Cream, Ocher, Eggshell White—
Walking Inside the Historic Ring

We are approaching the first district from the Ringstraße, the magnificent, multi-lane road that surrounds the innermost historical core of the city. Behind us is the Votivkirche and the swell of afternoon traffic on a cold Friday in December. We walk through Schottengasse toward the center of the first district. The sidewalk is narrow and there is a lot going on at eye level—the bright colors of coats, shopping bags, garbage cans, vehicles, signs, displays, and Christmas lights all catch the eye (Fig. 1). Street signs with red frames are mounted on the corners of the houses.

Fig. 1

What are the requirements for signs and advertisements?
Signs, neon signs, and stickers are assessed by the municipal department of architecture and urban design. "Advertising structures must be adapted to the townscape in terms of form, scale, and color." The requirements apply in particular to protected zones. Signs may only be installed on the ground floor or in business zones and the maximum surface area for push-in signs is 0.5 sqm. Individual letters are preferred to flat panels.[3] Flashing signs are not permitted.

Why do Vienna's street signs have a red border?
Since 1862, the nine districts of Vienna each had their own color for the border; the first district was red. The different shapes were also important for orientation: the oval signs indicated a radial street, i.e., a street leading away from the center, while the square signs indicated a tangential street. The system for designating and signposting Vienna's streets was developed by Michael Winkler.[4] The entrepreneur not only developed the system, but also produced the cast zinc signs in his factory. From 1920 on, the color red was used for all districts, as the number of districts had increased to nineteen since the incorporation in 1892. Starting in 1923, the signs were redesigned: Latin letters replaced the Fraktur script, in white on a blue background.[5] Since the 1980s, historical replicas have been repeatedly installed in the protection zones.

Fig. 2

When we reach Freyung, we raise our gaze. Above the dense, busy ground floor zone, the façades form a calm picture. The colors match tone on tone. Cream, limestone, beige, light gray, ocher, eggshell white (Fig. 2). The ornamentation and stucco on the façades stand out discreetly from the basic façade color. The deliberately light and restrained use of colors imparts a uniform, characteristic appearance to the entire inner city.

How do typical urban color palettes come about?
This has a lot to do with the geology and climate of a place. Many buildings in Vienna were built with Leitha lime (lime from the Leitha Mountains) or sand-lime brick (Fig. 3). The color of the lime was also used for paintwork. Bright colors were considered "provincial" during the late-nineteenth century in Vienna.[6] Other seemingly typical Viennese colors "Schönbrunn yellow" or "Otto Wagner green." However, these colors are often misunderstood. Schönbrunn Palace, which has also been colored pink and blue in the past, includes shades of yellow in ten different nuances. And the railings of the Otto Wagner stations were by no means always green—they have been repainted fifteen times in 115 years. The first green paint job dates back to the 1950s.[7]

Although subtle, the city center has its own character in colors with a high recognition value. It is part of

Fig. 3

Vienna's identity and international image, attracting thousands of tourists every year. The city center is generally characterized by people passing by—shoppers and tourists. In front of the Constitutional Court, there is a mountain of black garbage bags from the Christmas market, leaving traces of pre-Christmas consumption in the urban space. We hardly discover any places or corners that have been appropriated by residents.

Who protects the appearance of historic Vienna?
Since the 1972 amendment to the building code preserving the old town, the City of Vienna has been able to protect characteristic ensembles from demolition or alteration. The protection zones are not limited to the first district but include all those areas "that are important for preserving the identity and character of the city."[8] In total, this accounts for 8–9 percent of the entire building fabric. While the protection of ensembles is the responsibility of the city, the protection of monuments is the responsibility of the federal government.

Who are the people in the first district?
With around 16,000 people, the first district is the least populous district in Vienna, but at 55 square meters, it has the largest area per capita. In 1961, twice as many people lived here.[9] At the same time, the first district is the one with the most jobs—around 144,000 people work in companies, administration, and tourism.

Fig. 4

Near Tiefer Graben, we spot one of the few new buildings in the first district with a façade in various shades of brown. At first, we are surprised by the dark tones, but as we walk around the corner, we discover a historic building—the Mexican embassy—in a similar brown tone. The new building is color-coordinated with its surroundings. However, the smooth surface of the façade stands out, as almost all the other surrounding façades are finished in plaster or natural stone. Their rough surface creates a nuanced color spectrum through shadows, dirt, and unevenness.

> *Who has a say in the design of the façades?*
> "From a design perspective, a color can only be seen and evaluated in relation to its surroundings. The aim is to define a color palette that corresponds to the architecture and the immediate surroundings. Color combinations should be found that meet the wishes of the submitters as well as the requirements of the local cityscape."[10]
>
> Color schemes in the protection zones are subject to an assessment by MA 19, the Municipal Department for architecture and urban design. The study on the color design of historic façades in Vienna by architect and monument conservator Friedmund Hueber serves as a guideline. Using examples with happy or sad smileys, the study describes design measures for façades within the protection zone.[11]

On many corners, it is the infrastructural elements that catch the eye most strongly. Street signs such as a red "Stop," the bright blue pedestrian zone, or the Viennese dustbins with bright orange lettering—they defy the noble color palette of the old town and stand out due to their recognizable shape. A bright orange MA 48 refuse truck is just turning the corner at the Schulhof square (Fig. 4).

> *Why is the waste infrastructure orange?*
> Orange is considered the most visible color, even in fog or at dusk. The color is therefore used and worn on the high seas and in road traffic for safety reasons. MA 48—the municipal department 48 for waste management, street cleaning, and vehicle fleet—has generally used orange for its corporate identity. In addition to the work clothing and garbage carts, the Instagram page (@die48er), information sheets, and garbage bin labels are also orange. These slogans, which are now attached to 18,800 bins throughout Vienna, were selected in an online vote, including "Brauche mehr Input!" (Need more input) and "Volltreffer!" (Bull's eye!)[12]

The floor coverings vary—cobblestones, asphalt with curbs, large slabs. The cobblestones create a multitonal gray, varied color palette. Water, snow, and horse manure from horse-drawn carriages collect in the joints, while moss and weeds grow in other places. The stones and their nuanced colors create a pleasant leap in scale amid the monumental façades. One disadvantage, however, is that they make it difficult for people in wheelchairs, on bicycles, or with baby carriages to get around. Where cars drive, the city has filled the joints with a black substance. We cross the road and walk back in the direction of the purple subway line.

> *Who decides on the colors of the subway lines?*
> The colors of Vienna's subway lines are red (U1), violet (U2), orange (U3), green (U4), and brown (U6). The colors can also be found in numerous elements within the stations where they help with orientation, especially at junctions. The color of the new U5 line, whose construction began in 2018, was decided by online voting. Some 143,000 passengers took part, with 65 percent voting for turquoise.[13]

Half an hour and fifteen stops later, we get off at Seestadt Aspern.

Gray, Green, White—
Exploring the New Ring in the Periphery

Seestadt Aspern is an urban development area, which is currently under construction, in Vienna's 22nd district Donaustadt. Construction cranes dominate the scene (Fig. 5). Coming from the north, we walk across empty lots that are yet to be developed, toward the "new city." We are not the only strollers on

Fig. 5

this day, as the new roads between the construction sites are already being used as a running route or for walking the dog. The individual quarters of the new district are arranged around Asperner Ringstraße. As the main street, where all road users, whether pedestrians, cyclists or drivers, are treated equally in the future, it serves as the most important connecting element in the new district.

How did the two ring roads come about?
"Traditionally, ring roads define the outer areas of a city center and serve as transport links to which important arterial roads connect."[14] From 1858, Vienna's fortress wall, which had previously surrounded the entire inner city, was demolished. As a result, Vienna's Ringstraße was built on the extensive open spaces between the city center and the remaining districts, with numerous magnificent buildings and green spaces—such as the Burgtheater, the Votivkirche, and the Volksgarten. The new Aspern Ringstraße finds an important urban reference point in the Vienna Ringstraße, which was also conceived as a place of communication and connection. The *Partitur des öffentlichen Raums*, the planning manual for Seestadt Aspern, states: "The Ringstraße consists of several segments with different characters in terms of activities, building edges, and design of the street sections ... . Each district shows its best side towards the Ringstraße. The Ringstraße is the window to the city districts."[15]

Fig. 6

We stand on a field and look out over the growing city. From our vantage point, the color scheme of Seestadt Aspern appears quite uniform, as the façades of the buildings are largely designed in shades of gray, brown, beige, and sand with light or dark accents. Only individual buildings stand out of the color scheme, making the houses of the Baugruppen (communities for building together), Leuchtturm Seestadt, and Kolokation—which we know from our involvement with communal housing projects—look like bright splashes of color in the landscape (Fig. 6).

Why are the buildings by the Baugruppen colorful? Behind the purple façade of the "Kolokation am Seebogen" housing project, old and young live next door to each other with the aim of providing mutual support in everyday life. Freya Brandl, founding member of the Kolokation association, comments on the color of the house: "Ruth (also a member of the association) invited us to dinner, the menu was: rump steak with purple potatoes and red cabbage for the main course, crêpes with cranberry cream for dessert, accompanied by dark red wine. The table was set with a bouquet of purple tulips and the napkins were the same color. Everything had something to do with autumn, as did Kolokation itself"—which is probably why the house is also purple.[16] The green façade belongs to the communal housing project "Leuchtturm Seestadt." Felix Murnig, resident and member of the *Baugruppe*, explains that the green façade color was chosen by the

Fig. 7

founding group early on in the process because it corresponded to the idea and vision of a shared home. During the construction process, it turned out that a white façade would be more cost-effective, but the group still opted for a green house.[17]

Another strong color point in our field of vision is the area under the above-ground subway line (Fig. 7). The floor, wall surfaces, sports- and play-equipment are kept in vibrant shades of green, with only the galvanized City of Vienna bike racks breaking out of the color scheme. Like a green ribbon, the sports and play area for children, young people, and adults follows the line into the center of Seestadt.

How did this green ribbon come about?
The green ribbon is part of the Elinor-Ostrom-Park. The area along the subway line was integrated into the park concept as a multifunctional, weather-protected play and leisure zone (ball courts, water and bicycle playground, swing boats, boulder blocks, street workout and parkour facility, slackline area, and fitness mile). A participation process was organized for the design of the Elinor-Ostrom-Park from March to April 2017, in which citizens were able to express their personal opinions, suggestions and wishes. According to the City of Vienna: "The willingness to participate and the level of interest were high: the majority of respondents were particularly in favor of lots of

Fig. 8

green spaces, shady trees and fitness and sports facilities for young people and adults."[18]

The five- to seven-story buildings on both sides of the subway line are discreetly designed, with lighter and darker shades of brown characterizing their façades. The buildings on the construction site are each oriented toward a shared courtyard. We stop in an inner courtyard—natural stone paving in sandy tones, concrete walls with wooden seating elements, grasses, shrubs, and bushes in between (Fig. 8). We notice that the standardized Viennese elements of public space, such as galvanized bike racks and streetlamps, are missing. Instead, the lights, railings, garbage cans, and bike racks are powder-coated in a uniform dark gray. Façades, floor coverings, planting, and infrastructural elements are color-coordinated to create a uniform image in the courtyard.

Which design standards exist for public spaces?
In Austria, there are various planning instruments that define open space planning standards. For example, the location, size, and function of a public open space is defined in a zoning plan. The *Spielplatzverordnung* (playground ordinance) ensures that sufficient areas for outdoor play are created as part of residential construction projects. Another innovative planning instrument is *Partitur des öffentlichen Raums*. The process-oriented planning manual for the Seestadt Aspern provides guidelines for the programming and

Fig. 9

design of public urban spaces focusing on the fundamental needs of future residents. Public urban spaces have different purposes and are aimed at different target groups.

The walk takes us to the next construction site, where the courtyard is slightly elevated and can be reached via stairs and ramps. Low, freestanding concrete walls, a playing field with a yellow EPDM surface, small wooden houses, a sandpit with a watercourse and sun protection—this courtyard invites children to play. The surrounding buildings are once again pushed into the background by their subtly colored façades in light gray and white. We leave the inner courtyard via a staircase, which is adjoined by a colorful house wall that is unlike any other (Fig. 9). The wall is divided into many areas—gray, white, orange, light, and dark green. In each of these areas there is a different drawing—sometimes the scene of a stroller, sometimes elements of a bicycle, or a still life of a fruit bowl. The mural is by artist Paul Riedmüller, who, in addition to canvases, also paints blank walls under the name "Perkup," usually as a collective with colleagues.

How was this mural created?
Paul Riedmüller: In this case, the Oxymoron Galerie—a gallery that focuses on exhibitions of graffiti, street art, and art in urban spaces—announced a competition for the design of the wall. My sketch ended up being selected from the submissions. Of course, the sketch was then

Fig. 10

adapted and refined.[19] But the process was relatively short, because after a few months the date was set, and we started painting.

And how long does it take to finish the picture?
Paul Riedmüller: Actually, I always like to do things like this collectively. We are a crew of five people. The mural in Seestadt is by far the biggest wall I've ever done on my own. Nevertheless, I had support from various sides during the process. The company organized the paints and the lifting platform in advance. And to speed up the process, I sometimes worked with projections at night, which was helped by a friend who does event projections. So, the first two days were spent priming, painting surfaces, and sketching.[20] I then spent seven days actually painting.

How do people perceive painting in public spaces?
Paul Riedmüller: It's amazing how much feedback I get when I paint on the street and how many people think it's cool—even older people. I often paint still lifes or spatial motifs, which everyone thinks is great. It's nice to know that you can make someone's life, an everyday scene, a little more beautiful—that's why I like painting murals so much.[21]

Critique, Signal, Identify—
What Do Colors Do in Public Space?

Looking at murals and graffiti opens up colorful playing fields in urban space beyond the classic surface design of walls and floors. They can be found at the skate park under the subway line in Seestadt, on the Danube Canal, on firewalls, on walls at Schwendermarkt and Yppenplatz, and in countless other places in Vienna (Fig. 10). Graffiti are like little messages that people leave for each other. It's about the appropriation of surfaces in color, about pointing to something—people exchange ideas by painting, so to speak.

Where in the city are you actually allowed to paint? "Graffiti is one of the most visible and certainly one of the most discussed forms of expression in youth culture ... . In many cities, graffiti is seen as a purely criminal act that can onlybe countered by rigorous bans."[22] With the Wienerwand Project, the City of Vienna is taking a different approach and creating legal graffiti areas to support this form of art. The aim is to promote dialogue between artists and the public. The website www.wienerwand.at provides an overview map of all legal graffiti areas in Vienna, as well as the rules that users must adhere to. The graffiti areas are marked by the "Wiener Taube"—a relief of a dove that is usually already painted over with many layers of paint.

However, if you take a walk around Vienna, you will also find numerous house walls that have been illegally tagged. These graffiti usually point to a grievance, such as the vacancy of a house, and thus illustrate a critical engagement with urban space. It is the task of a democratic society to negotiate public space, to clarify needs, to appropriate parts of the city, and to consciously help shape them.

Colors in urban space are part of this appropriation process. At the same time, a closer look reveals many rules of social coexistence and ongoing processes of democratic negotiation. The stroll revealed to us the complexity of Vienna's colors. By "looking" closely and questioning as we walked, we opened up "new perspectives"—we discovered the colors of appropriation in countless graffiti, got to know the history of the nineteenth century in the subtleties of monumental renovation, and consciously perceived colorful ideas in the design of a new district. We have seen that colors everywhere also help with communication, orientation, and safety, as demonstrated by the countless street signs and guidance systems.

Colors in urban spaces are an expression of identity, history, and design. They shape the collective image of a city like the color palette of lime. At the same time, their diversity indicates the social heterogeneity of a city. Colors in urban space can have a powerful radiance, like the Ringstraße on the day of Vienna Pride, when an otherwise traffic-dominated street becomes a rainbow-colored festival.

Notes

1 Lucius Burckhardt, Kulturbeutel, Organ der Spaziergangswissenschaft, Gesamthochschule Kassel, Seminar Wahrnehmung & Verkehr, Kassel 1993.

2 See www.stadtstuecke.at. Everyone is invited to join in and share city pieces on the platform.

3 City of Vienna, Architecture and Urban design (MA 19), "Geschäftsaufschrift, Leuchtreklame und Steckschilder—Begutachtung," accessed January 10, 2023, https://www.wien.gv.at/amtshelfer/bauen-wohnen/stadtentwicklung/werbeanlagen/geschaeftsaufschrift.html.

4 Michael Winkler, *Winkler's Orientierungsplan für die k. k. Reichs- und Residenzstadt Wien und seine acht umliegenden Vorstadt-Bezirke* (Wien, 1862).

5 Sándor Békési, "Orientation, standardization and control," September 11, 2020, accessed January 3, 2023, https://magazin.wienmuseum.at/die-beschilderung-und-umbenennung-der-strassen.

6 Friedmund Hueber, quoted in Elisabeth Gerstendorfer, "Die Angst der Architekten vor der Farbe," *Die Presse*, December 3, 2011.

7 Johannes Luxner, "Sehgewohnheiten und Wirklichkeit," orf.at, December 30, 2017, accessed March 11, 2023, https://orf.at/v2/stories/2419747/2419744/.

8 Felix Czeike, "Schutzzone," in: *Historisches Lexikon der Stadt Wien*, Vol. 5, 169.

9 City of Vienna, "Bevölkerung nach Bezirken 2005 bis 2020," accessed January 10, 2023, https://www.wien.gv.at/statistik/bevoelkerung/tabellen/bevoelkerung-bez-zr.html; City of Vienna, "Erwerbstätige am Arbeitsort Wien nach Bezirken 2017," accessed January 10, 2023, https://www.wien.gv.at/statistik/arbeitsmarkt/tabellen/bezirke-erwerbstaetige-aest.html; see also, Martin Putschögl, Bernadette Redl, and Franziska Zoidl, "Den Ersten im Blick: Living in the City of Vienna," *Der Standard*, November 4, 2022.

10 City of Vienna, "Farbgestaltung—Begutachtung," accessed December 15, 2022, https://www.wien.gv.at/amtshelfer/bauen-wohnen/stadtentwicklung/baulicheanlagen/farbgestaltung.html.

11 Friedmund Hueber, "Farbgestaltung historischer Fassaden in Wien," 2008, 76.

12 Wien Erleben, "Die Mistkübel von Wien," accessed January 4, 2023, https://wien-erleben.com/die-mistkuebel-von-wien/.

13 "Linie U5 wird türkis," orf.at, August 28, 2014, accessed March 11, 2023, https://wien.orf.at/v2/news/stories/2665321/.

14 Gehl Architects, "Stadtentwicklung und Stadtplanung: Partitur des öffentlichen Raums—Planungshandbuch Aspern Seestadt," published by Magistratsabteilung 18 and Wien 3420 Aspern Development AG, Vienna 2009, 40.

15 Gehl Architects, "Stadtentwicklung und Stadtplanung: Partitur des öffentlichen Raums," 41.

16 E-Mail from Freya Brandl to Rebekka Hirschberg, Vienna, March 13, 2023.

17 Interview with Felix Murnig conducted by Anna Jäger, Vienna, January 12, 2023.

18 City of Vienna, "Elinor-Ostrom-Park," accessed January 4, 2023, https://www.wien.gv.at/umwelt/parks/anlagen/elinorostrom.html.

19 Interview with Paul Riedmüller conducted by Rebekka Hirschberg and Anna Jäger, Vienna, November 4, 2022.

20 Ibid.

21 Ibid.

22 City of Vienna, https://www.wienerwand.at, accessed January 4, 2023.

High-Tech, Big Tech, Technicolor

Adam Sherman

321

Fig. 1

The Starship in the Loop

Drenched in color, the atrium of Chicago's Thompson Center immediately overwhelms. This urban room soars to an astonishing height, drawing the eye up seventeen stories. Two exposed elevator cores tower overhead as twelve glass elevators glide up and down, their cables lagging behind.

Light blue and salmon panels of metal and glass form curved walls that encircle the space. A sprawling web of red-painted steel articulates all of the elements in the atrium; this structural network covers the full height of the stepped glass façade, spans the inclined glass roof, suspends staircases, and frames elevator shafts (Fig. 1).

The atrium of the Thompson Center is nothing short of dazzling. The kaleidoscopic interior choreographs a multitude of heterogeneous parts—many of them moving—into a single, centripetal organization. The atrium's gravitational pull even seems to extend outside the building to attract neighboring towers, which peer inside through the enormous glass façade.

But, while showcasing a frivolous spirit, at times the atrium is downright tacky. The pale colors that surround the room are faded and dull. The floor tiles that articulate the atrium's radial geometry seem straight out of a shopping mall. The cheap-stores and fast-food restaurants that line the interior disrupt the possibility of gravitas.

To step into the Thompson Center is to enter an architectural spectacle both daring and dated.

Fig. 2

At least this was the experience, until the atrium closed for renovation in 2022.

Completed in 1985, the James R. Thompson Center opened as an Illinois state government office building in the Loop in Downtown Chicago (Fig. 2). Originally named the State of Illinois Center, the building promised to consolidate many state government offices in Chicago under one roof and serve as a secondary capitol building in Illinois's most populous city.[1] Helmut Jahn—a German architect who had emigrated to Chicago and started his own practice—designed the building, which was completed during the tenure of Illinois Governor James R. Thompson, for whom the building was eventually named.

The building was a statement piece, intended to celebrate the state through architecture. Its exuberance was meant to inspire the people of Illinois and connect them with their government. Proponents of the building's bravado threw around clichés about optimism, dignity, and accessibility. Behind all that glass lay a stale metaphor equating material transparency with state transparency. Jahn argued that a non-neutral color palette was appropriate specifically because this was a government building,[2] though his Athletic Facility at Saint Mary's College—completed eight years earlier—also features prominent red trusses.

Jahn drew from historical references to attempt to render the building an appropriate house of government and an exemplar of tradition, grandeur, and stability. The cylindrical atrium—rising from the ground, piercing through the roof, and cut at an angle—was

Fig. 3

his reinterpretation of the dome of the rotunda of Henry Ives Cobb's Chicago Federal Building of 1905.[3] Granite panels, though used sparingly, give a touch of firmness befitting a temple of democracy. An exterior colonnade at the building's base rounds out the classical quotations,[4] keeping the Starship—as the building has come to be known—grounded (Fig. 3).

But the most salient architectural reference for this city within a city was the shopping mall. Below the office floors, Jahn inserted a base with two floors of retail space and an underground food court (whose sounds and smells would waft up into the rest of the building). Some of the public-facing spaces, such as the CTA Metro Station and Department of Motor Vehicles, did provide important city and state services. But the wide selection of stores and restaurants, known together as the Atrium Mall, simply carried the commercial conditions of contemporary urban life into the Thompson Center. Jahn did not distinguish this administrative space from the rest of the city; rather, he integrated the two seamlessly.[5] Whether cynical or pragmatic, his plan to draw the public into this public building—and keep the atrium bustling and lively throughout the day—centered on the attractions of shops and restaurants.[6]

Accompanying the variety of retail spaces was a considerable amount of signage. But what was remarkable about the Thompson Center was how easily the dizzying atrium integrated billboards and storefronts into its totalizing environment. Here, the visual culture of consumerism was not unsightly detritus or a foreign parasite, sucking the life out of its

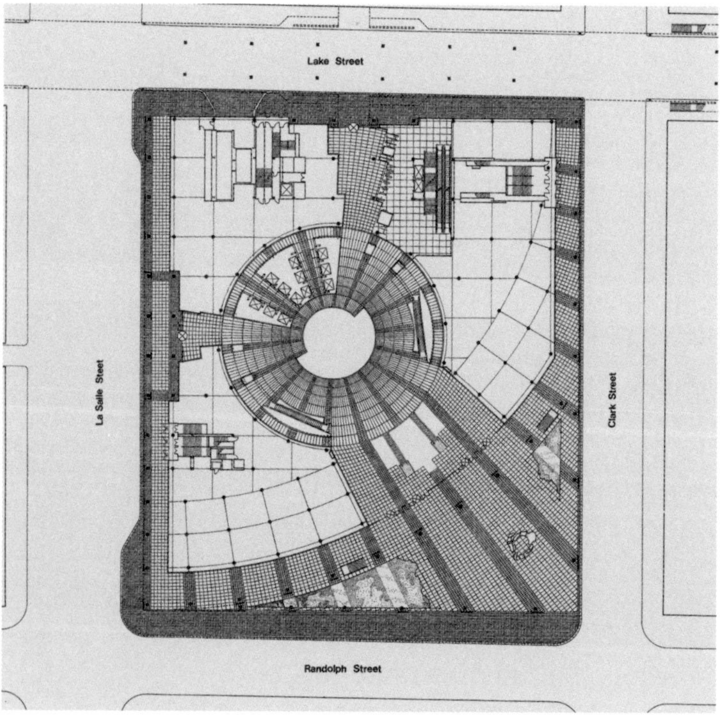

Fig. 4

architectural host. Rather, this signage was integral—if not subordinate—to the architectural space it inhabited.

The cylindrical atrium, though systematic on its own, lies amid a hodgepodge of other gestures (Fig. 4), all housed within a truncated cone, trimmed asymmetrically on three different sides (Fig. 5). Covering this inscrutable volume with curved glass came with an astronomical price tag, forcing heavy value engineering. To cut costs, the design team swapped out richly colored, insulating glass with a pale, single-paned alternative.[7]

However, the thermal performance of this cheaper glass was severely lacking. To adequately condition a building with so much glazing, engineers introduced a complicated system that would produce ice slush in the basement overnight and then use the slush to cool air that would circulate through the building during the day. Even for standard operation, the building needed to consider the daily timetable of energy pricing: the system made the ice slush at night because that was when electricity was cheapest.[8] Far from self-sufficient, the building was deeply entangled in both inefficient energy practice and the economic apparatus governing that energy usage.

Already by the first summer of operation, high temperatures were impossible for the climate control system to handle. The building heated up into a sauna, forcing government employees to resort to a number of messy, ad-hoc solutions to make their office space habitable. Newspapers began publishing scandalous photos of umbrellas and industrial

Fig. 5

fans scattered among the cubicles in this supposedly state-of-the-art center.[9] Though the addition of cooling towers eventually solved these thermal issues,[10] the controversy had already wounded the building's reputation.

The building also suffered from other maintenance problems. In 2009, a large granite piece weighing over 250 kilograms fell off one of the building's exterior columns. The accident prompted the subsequent removal of all of the colonnade's stone,[11] signifying a (perhaps too precise) metaphor for the crumbling of democracy. This was not Jahn's first brush with near catastrophe—a large portion of the roof of his Kemper Arena had collapsed in 1979 due to a poorly designed water drainage system.[12]

By 2015, management and maintenance costs of the Thompson Center had grown too great for the state to sustain. Illinois needed a solution and put the building up for sale. Governor Bruce Rauner, a Republican and former private equity investor, even expressed openness to full demolition of the building.[13] Preservationists panicked and placed the Thompson Center near the top of lists that inventory the country's most endangered buildings.[14]

Eventually, in 2021, the state found a buyer in the developer Prime Realty, who agreed to carry out a renovation and save the Thompson Center from demolition. Jahn's firm, set to manage the renovation, released initial renderings that proposed a possible future for the building, with a drastic toning-down of the color scheme.[15] The images show a new atrium, organized by a large, curved glass volume (à la

Norman Foster's Apple stores), that would shed the blue, salmon, and red. Only the green of trees placed behind the façade and around the atrium would punctuate the sterility of this glass and steel environment. Even in this twenty-first century update, the tendency to use color in an attempt to offset assumptions about the Thompson Center remains the same: red trusses made a drab office seem playful, so green vegetation could make this inefficient behemoth seem sustainable.

In 2022, Google finally emerged as the new tenant, agreeing to occupy the entire building with 2,000 employees. The deal was music to the ears of politicians like Mayor Lori Lightfoot, who celebrated the news as "a milestone in Chicago history."[16] But despite the apparent interest in maintaining the spirit of the original design, as expressed by Google and Jahn's firm, Prime Realty still rejected a petition to add the Thompson Center to the National Register of Historic Places.[17] Because of this, the ultimate questions of what the building will look like and how it will function once Google moves in remain unanswered.

The Perfect Tenant

When tech companies move their offices or stores into historic buildings, they sometimes create a visual wrinkle in time. Think, say, of the anachronistic landing of a fleet of MacBooks and their attendant Geniuses with the opening of a new Apple store in the Main Concourse of Grand Central Station in 2011. Google's move into the Thompson Center seems somehow more fitting, partially because the search engine's coders will be working in an office space that is just forty years old.

But there are other, deeper reasons for this congruity of property and occupant. More convincingly than state government, Google can assume a public posture of informality that resonates with the devil-may-care attitude of the building's design. And given how Google's multicolored logo is already so deeply entrenched in the broader cultural consciousness, the atrium, if its colors are kept, would amount to seventeen stories of spatial marketing.

Underpinning the Thompson Center's original medley of state and commercial programs was the notion that engagement with government should not feel like a descent into the grayness of bureaucracy but rather an ascent into a world of color and consumption. On the way to make a filing at the Illinois Pollution Control Board, you could also buy shaving cream at Walgreens, get a trim at SuperCuts, and eat a Cheesy Gordita Crunch at Taco Bell. This assertion, that fun activities can spice up boring desk jobs, is the same underlying selling point for the free perks that employees receive at tech offices. How convenient that Google can move into a space already capable of accommodating the variety of amenities the company offers to its workers.

In a political climate that demanded austerity in public architecture, Jahn's atrium had its detractors. When pressed about this supposed "waste of space" as tall as the building itself, Governor Thompson would defend the interior by responding: "Would you rather I filled up the building with bureaucrats?"[18] But this enormous cylindrical void fits well into a model that already defines so many new, flashy tech campuses: a large, open space with a clear geometry. Just look at Foster + Partners' Apple Park (a big ring), NBBJ's Amazon Spheres (three big spheres), and BIG + Heatherwick Studio's Google Bay View (three big tents).

The End of Government

Spatially empty yet visually full to the brim, the atrium of the Thompson Center is the epitome of Frederic Jameson's "postmodern hyperspace."[19] Color dematerializes the space while articulated structure excites the eye. Exposed elevators are substitutes for movement in an office building where workers spend their days inert, seated at desks. Paul Goldberger, the critic who originally reviewed the Thompson Center for *The New York Times*, writes that the phantasmagoria of the building amounts to "architecture on amphetamines."[20]

Acknowledging Jameson and Goldberger, Jonathan Solomon sees the insertion of government services within the colorful theatrics of this retail environment as "both empowering in the access it promises the individual and disturbing in the pervasiveness it allows for an atomized and distributed State apparatus."[21] But if the Thompson Center is a Trojan horse that snuck government into the space of commerce, the building also snuck commerce into the space of government. The atrium's juxtaposition of storefronts and restaurants alongside state offices reinforces the notion of the "citizen consumer,"[22] whose engagement with government inevitably coincides with the act of buying stuff.

A precedent for a public institution whose architecture celebrates high-tech, consumerist spectacle also exists in the Centre Pompidou, completed in 1977 by Renzo Piano and Richard Rogers. The Thompson Center and the Centre Pompidou share many obvious similarities: the expression of structure, the embrace of color, and the celebration of circulation. Even their shared name ("center") gestures at the wide range of activities that can take place in these multi-purpose structures, to which the old monikers of "museum" or "government building" simply no longer apply. Both buildings were products of a moment when state institutions had to respond to a rapidly transforming public sphere defined by new technological regimes and media cultures.

Jean Baudrillard posits that crowds flocked to the Pompidou because the building transformed art into entertainment.[23] At the Pompidou, consumer capitalism and mass culture swallowed up the notion of a museum. The Centre Pompidou—stripped to the bones, inundated with media, and obsessed with the didactic display of its own flows and networks—was the logical conclusion of an impoverished cultural life. If, for Baudrillard, the Centre Pompidou marked the end of culture, then does the Thompson Center not mark the end of government?

Fig. 6

The sale of the Thompson Center is significant because the building's *raison d'être* centered on its symbolic celebration of what public architecture could look like, carrying the spirit of a city and a state. The specific story of this architecture relied on the specificity of its owner. At the Thompson Center's 1985 opening ceremony, a huge banner reading "A BUILDING FOR YEAR 2000" hung down in the atrium (Fig. 6). The building may have had its eyes set fifteen years into the future, but only thirty years into its lifespan, the Thompson Center had already proved unfit for its original occupants.

Striving for bold expression with reckless abandon, Jahn ambitiously designed a building that was over-budget and under-engineered, with inefficiencies impossible for a state client to manage. But while this technological system was ill-suited for the building's public owner, so was the technological aesthetic. Jahn liberally applied visual marks of high-tech: the architectural language of late capitalism and *lingua franca* of an increasingly globalized culture that values private interests over those of the general public.[24]

In his own writing, Jahn positions his practice against the movements of Late Modernism and Postmodernism and situates his work at the intersection of many considerations—historical, technological, formal, and programmatic—that he believes distinguish him from his contemporaries.[25] We might then consider two other American government buildings completed around the same time as the Thompson Center, by prominent architects associated with these other movements: I. M. Pei's Dallas City Hall, completed in 1978, and Michael Graves's Portland Building, completed in 1982. Dated as these municipal buildings may seem now, they both sought to represent the state in their own ways. Pei chose a less efficient floor area distribution to extend a public plaza below an impressive concrete cantilever, while Graves added oversized pilasters and other classical elements to evoke the symbolism of government (more explicitly than Jahn at the Thompson Center). These visual claims of Dallas City Hall and the Portland Building, if not inherently public, at the very least bear little association with malls or corporate office buildings—the architecture of the production and consumption of private wealth. The conversion of these other government buildings into facilities for eBay or Amazon seems unlikely.

Consider now two icons of corporate culture built at the same time (and in a similar style) as the Thompson Center: Norman Foster's HSBC Building, which opened in 1985, and Richard Rogers's Lloyd's Building, which opened a year later. With massive atria, articulated structure, and expressed circulation, these buildings use many of the same high-tech tricks that are present at the Thompson Center. But unlike the singularity of Illinois state government in Chicago, the financial institutions that own Foster's and Rogers's towers are a dime a dozen in their respective cities of Hong Kong and London. Thus, the efforts to distinguish these corporate tenants through high-tech architecture amount to little more than a narcissism of small differences.

Jahn may have envisioned the Thompson Center as an attempt to elevate government, to represent it as something exceptional. But in carrying out this fantasy, he utilized an architectural language associated with the increasing subordination of the state to the corporation. Viewed through this lens, the Thompson Center's eventual privatization seems like an inevitability, practically anticipated by the architecture itself. It took almost forty years, but the Thompson Center may have finally found its fated tenant.

Notes

1 Jonathan D. Solomon, "Helmut Jahn's James R. Thompson Center and the Aesthetics of Postmodern Citizenship," *The Avery Review*, no. 19 (November 2016), https://averyreview.com/issues/issue-19/aesthetics-of-postmodern-citizenship, 1–3.
2 Nathan Eddy, "Starship Chicago," Vimeo, 2017, accessed June 10, 2024, https://vimeo.com/241413433.
3 Lynn Becker, "The Rebuilding Process," *Chicago Reader*, July 31, 2003, https://chicagoreader.com/arts-culture/the-rebuilding-process.
4 Solomon, "Helmut Jahn's James R. Thompson Center and the Aesthetics of Postmodern Citizenship."
5 Ibid.
6 Paul Goldberger, "Futuristic State Office Building Dazzles Chicago," *The New York Times*, July 22, 1985, https://www.nytimes.com/1985/07/22/arts/futuristic-state-office-building-dazzles-chicago.html.
7 Becker, "The Rebuilding Process."
8 "Thompson Center," Chicago Architecture Center, accessed June 10, 2024, https://www.architecture.org/learn/resources/buildings-of-chicago/building/thompson-center.
9 Becker, "The Rebuilding Process."
10 Eddy, "Starship Chicago."
11 Blair Kamin, "Thompson Center to Shed the Granite," *Chicago Tribune*, October 15, 2009, https://www.chicagotribune.com/news/breaking/chi-thompson-center-granite-problems-20140813-story.html.
12 "The Story of the Kemper Arena Roof Collapse," *KC Yesterday*, https://kcyesterday.com/articles/kemper-arena-roof-collapse#:~:text=The%20Collapse,stress%20of%20the%20weather%20conditions.
13 Blair Kamin, "Spare Jahn's Thompson Center from Rauner's Death Sentence," *Chicago Tribune*, October 14, 2015, https://www.chicagotribune.com/news/breaking/ct-thompson-center-kamin-met-1015-20151014-column.html.
14 Blair Kamin, "Thompson Center Placed on Top-11 List of Nation's Most Endangered Historic Places," *Chicago Tribune*, May 30, 2019, https://www.chicagotribune.com/columns/blair-kamin/ct-biz-thompson-center-kamin-0530-story.html.

15 Tom Ravenscroft, “Helmut Jahn’s Postmodern Thompson Center Saved from Demolition,” *Dezeen*, December 15, 2021, https://www.dezeen.com/2021/12/15/helmut-jahn-thompson-center-saved-demolition.

16 David Roeder, “Google Taking over Thompson Center from the State,” *Chicago Sun Times*, July 28, 2022, https://chicago.suntimes.com/2022/7/27/23280587/google-thompson-center.

17 Pansy Schulman, “Nomination of Chicago’s Thompson Center to National Register Blocked by New Owner,” *Architectural Record*, March 20, 2023, https://www.architecturalrecord.com/articles/16153-nomination-of-chicagos-thompson-center-to-national-register-blocked-by-new-owner.

18 Eddy, “Starship Chicago.”

19 Frederic Jameson, *Postmodernism, or, The Cultural Logic of Late Capitalism* (Durham: Duke University Press, 1991).

20 Goldberger, “Futuristic State Office Building Dazzles Chicago.”

21 Solomon, “Aesthetics of Postmodern Citizenship.”

22 Douglas Spencer, “Festivals of Circulation: Neoliberal Architectures of Culture, Commerce and Education,” in *The Architecture of Neoliberalism: How Contemporary Architecture Became an Instrument of Control and Compliance* (London: Bloomsbury Academic, 2016), 111–37.

23 Jean Baudrillard and Sheila Faria Glaser, “The Beaubourg Effect: Implosion and Deterrence,” in *Simulacra and Simulation* (Ann Arbor: The University of Michigan Press, 1994), 61–74.

24 Edwin Heathcote, “How ‘High Tech’ Became the Architectural Style of Globalisation,” *Financial Times*, March 23, 2018, https://www.ft.com/content/92d5063a-277d-11e8-9274-b13fccdc744.

25 Joachim Andreas Joedicke, Helmut Jahn, and Peter Green, “Toward a New Synthesis,” in *Helmut Jahn: Design Einer Neuen Architektur = Design of a New Architecture = Design d’une Architecture Nouvelle* (Stuttgart: Karl Krämer Verlag, 1986), 9–11.

We Paint Ourselves a Room

Institut Vierzehn

Color is a carrier of sentiment and atmosphere. It can influence spaces just as much as the people who inhabit them. Color is abstract, but at the same time very specific. It can make rooms appear smaller or larger, play with perspectives, and direct our gaze. Color is rational, but it is also emotional and actually very complex.

Often neglected in architecture, the Institut Vierzehn is committed to color and dedicated an entire weekend to the spatial effect of color. Through collective testing, experimentation, and independent work, architecture students addressed the topic and brought a vacant building in Graz back to life. These results show the diverse ways in which color can be used in interior spaces.

Guided by the special characteristics of the individual rooms, eight different room concepts were created that respond individually to the existing building.

The Blue Room (Fig. 1, 2) is completely covered in one color. The color scheme is intended to create atmosphere. It is an attempt to equalize the characteristics of all existing materials. The prevailing lack of hierarchy creates a new sense of space. The equal value of all surfaces generates a feeling of immersion. At the same time, the blue color deliberately draws the focus to the window frames, creating a visual axis to the outside. The yellow-colored leaves of the trees enhance the contrast between the interior and exterior spaces, breaking up the equivalence between them.

In the Large Room (Fig. 3), we playfully worked against the fear of the white wall. The individual color elements function without any connection, entirely on their own terms. They understand, respond to, or ignore the existing situation. It is a game of contrasts.

The Toilet (Fig. 4) is cramped in the middle of the house. Without access to natural light, pink plays with the effect of the existing shadows. The friendliness of the color softens the darkness in the small room and underlines the character of the shadows. The abstract is emphasized and underlined here.

A similar principle is repeated in the Entrance Area of the house (Fig. 5). When the basement door is open, the white color makes it seem as though the shadow of the door on the floor has almost disappeared. The magenta-colored door forms a rectangle with the surrounding outline, once again playing with color and perspective. Only when the door is closed does the white negative space appear, which looks like an imprint of the closed door. It is a superimposition across several levels: the wall and rear wall, the ceiling, the floor, and the door.

Complementing the existing building, the color in the Bathroom (Fig. 6) works with what is already present. The existing is emphasized and expanded. Consistently, areas are created that differ only in color and pattern. The purpose of the existing configuration is ignored in order to create equivalence.

The red of the staircase (Fig. 7) has been extended to the entire stairwell. It is a further attempt to achieve a lack of hierarchy through using color. The room appears as a whole, without any consideration for individual functions and materials.

With a room height of 1.90 meters, the Green–Orange Room (Fig. 8) in the attic initially appeared very compact, perhaps despite (or because of) its size. By working with color in perspective, the room was given an imaginary, completed gable. Not just the optical illusion, but the contrasting selection of colors creates an expanded sense of space and changes the atmosphere.

The same concept was used to change the perspective of the Yellow–Purple Room (Fig. 9). The distortion of the spatial perspective results in a room-within-a-room, creating division through the use of complementary colors.

Initially conceived as an intensive exploration of the craft of painting, the majority of the students took an architectural approach and focused on the spatial effects of color. By playing, testing, and experimenting, they developed interior concepts which demonstrated that color should never be the last element to be considered in a design process.

Institut Vierzehn

Text:
Lea Schuiki

Photos:
Ingo Candussi, Gregor Klepatsch, and Maximilian Schlichtinger

Participants:
Blue room: Mona Kainrath, Lea Schuiki, Laura Thießen, and David Pöll; *Large room:* Fabian Steinberger; *Toilet:* Jasmin Monschein; *Entrance:* Gregor Klepatsch; *Bathroom:* Beatrice Raith, and Eleonora Schuler; *Red Staircase:* Momo Canzian, Tobias Hirtler; *Green-Orange room:* Anna-Maria Daniel, Lena Höll, Martin Kern, and Stefan Schenkel; *Yellow-Purple room:* Pia Pollak, Ingo Candussi, Theresa Hammerl, and Lois Stoisser

Fig. 1

Fig. 2

Fig. 3

Fig. 4

Fig. 5

Fig. 6

Fig. 7

Fig. 8

We Have Been Thinking a Lot About Red and Green Lately

Ajna and Adna Babahmetović

We have been thinking a lot about red and green lately. So much so that we started imagining our architecture in red and green, too. We wondered, why? The first logical step seemed to be the examination of our reference pools. Here, we must insert a disclaimer: our reference pool is, of course, not universal. It is shaped by a moment in time, an interface of our education, the context in which we work, the algorithms that are being created for us and for our architect friends. Perpetually, these references are being remixed and poured back into us all.

For example, we often reach out to the Swiss competition repositories. Since there is usually a rendering required (unlike Austrian competitions) it is easy to quickly scan through and catch up on the trends. Trends are more legible in competitions—non-built projects, projects on paper—where choices are made instinctively and quickly, without the immediate pressure of real-life consequences. We scanned one of the Swiss websites, in particular the competition results section, and roughly one-third of the winning proposals in 2022 contained either red, green, or both colors.[1] Two of our own competition proposals from the past two years were also in red and green.

If in need of curated references or the comfort of an algorithm, we turn to Instagram. Carefully assembled accounts—kind of obscure, yet popular enough—continually repost and repeat others' (as well as their own) photos, shaping the very specific aesthetic sensibilities we share with our friends. Scanning one of these reveals that, for example, Lilitt Bollinger's

Wohnatelierhaus (with its green stained wood—outside and inside) has been reposted three times on the same account, attracting more likes every time, the last post with around 8,000. Mariana de Delás's red window popped up on more accounts, generating more than 24,000 likes on this one.[2] While we are aware that many different factors contribute to the "virality" of these projects, we believe that color remains one of the prominent ones, easiest to detect, copy, and swiftly reuse in one's own projects.

After this brief investigation into the roots of our fascination, we wondered where the need for the examination even stemmed from. Today almost every color imaginable is possible in architecture. Yet, amid this abundance of color, there is still a looming feeling of dishonesty, even shame in deliberately using color, which is essentially perceived as unnecessary, a pure decoration, masking the true nature of the material. If it does not fulfill a function, why is it there?

A color discourse in architecture can usually be reduced to the question of whether color is weakening/eliminating or strengthening the bond between objects and the materials they are made of—or whether it is completely arbitrary.[3] As Gordon Shrigley writes: "does the color have a material relation or a rhetorical relation with the object it is being painted on?"[4]

We believe that red and green always have either one or both, and this is where their appeal and apparent self-evidence lies.

Let us start with red. One of the oldest pigments, red ocher or red earth has been used since prehistoric times—the first drawings found in early caves were painted using this pigment. Red earth is actually iron oxide, which can be found in abundance in the Earth's mantle. Iron oxide is a compound that comes to life when iron, oxygen, and water mix. So, the materials, coming from the Earth's crust, are red-colored because of iron oxide. That is why clay—and therefore bricks—have their distinctive red earthy hue. Fast forward to today: steel is an alloy of iron and carbon, and sometimes other additions. Used as a building material, steel needs to be protected from corrosion, since iron—in contact with oxygen and water—oxidizes to produce rust.

One of the most popular protective primers is Red Oxide Primer: it contains iron oxide and is one of the most widespread rust protections for ferrous metals. This is a fine example of material relation—iron is found in the object, and the paint itself. This further evolved into a symbolic relation, where red-colored steel established itself as a valid representation of steel, the material. We do not perceive it as overly unnatural, or fake. Rather, it strengthens the bond between steel and painting instead of weakening it.

Wood has no material connection to iron oxide, but there is a historic and highly symbolic one. Henry Dreyfuss once asked several of his colleagues why barns are painted red. He got many different answers (like, for example, that it is because of Christmas cards), all of them partly true. But the answer closest to the truth was probably that of Eero Saarinen—who connected the origins to the famous Swedish falu red.[5] The mine in the city of Falun in Sweden started producing residue at the end of the sixteenth century—this residue, which also contained iron oxide, proved to be a great anti-weathering paint when mixed with rye flour and linseed oil. Moreover, since brick houses were still reserved for the rich, painting wood in red seemed like a great alternative.[6] So, red paint protected wood and, while trying to imitate or fake the brick, created an honest material of its own—red wood. In the past twenty years, synthetic paints for wood have been further developed to be non-toxic and their popularity has grown immensely, which is why we see colored wood façades everywhere today.[7]

Another fitting example for this hypothesis is red concrete. It gained popularity only in recent years, mostly because of the very high costs of its production.[8] The concrete is colored with, of course, iron oxide particles. This is what gives it that synthetic, unnatural material "warmth" and earthiness—quite literally. One could say that concrete also engages in cosplay as brick. As such, it is imbued with symbolic power, showing that this choice of material can never be arbitrary or neutral.

The concrete of Gigon/Guyer's Switching Station in Zurich, built between 1997 and 1999, has also been colored with red oxide pigment. All the houses and objects in the surrounding area had a brownish-reddish patina, caused by the brake dust from the nearby train tracks. (The particles causing this discoloration were, of course, iron oxides). The architects decided to color the building with the same pigment, anticipating its patinated (polluted) destiny.[9] Red concrete refrains from mimicking brick, or even nature itself, in favor of adapting to its industrial surroundings, namely the railway infrastructure. Inevitably, focusing on the present and anticipating the future also brings the past to light. This narrative beautifully exposes the origins, naturalness, and ubiquitousness of the color red.

For the extension of the Reinhart Collection, Gigon/Guyer used a similar tactic. To ensure the new addition aligned with the existing Römerholz Villa—with its green roof flashing, drainpipes, window shutters, and moss—they again mixed concrete with dust. This time, it was a combination of Jura limestone and copper, both two of the primary materials used in the existing villa. When combined, these powders caused a quick oxidation process, coloring the concrete green. The concrete, once again, blends into its surroundings, embarking on a "journey through time."[10] But instead of heading toward the future, it returns to the past. Here, it cosplays as material whose patina is green, a color that has become emblematic of the act of aging itself.

Patinated copper is, apart from stone, one of the rare materials whose color is naturally green. Again, this patina is a rust protection, which forms over time on the surface of copper when exposed to the weather. Used since ancient times, this green hue became embedded in the collective consciousness—as a symbol of aging, but also protection, durability, and beauty. As such, we would argue that green's rhetorical or symbolic relation to objects precedes and shapes its material relation to them.

In an anecdote told by Jan De Vylder, he reveals how he started using the green his office became known for. Upon arrival at the construction site, he noticed a constructor was painting a metal beam green even though another color had been specified. When asked why, the constructor explained it was a protective coat, to be followed by the desired color. But in the end, De Vylder decided to stick with the green, finding it beautiful.[11] We wondered: could it be that the green was beautiful because it seemed to be an obvious choice for steel? Was it the wrong color covering exactly the right material? Was it the embrace of the unavoidable dailiness of green?[12]

If we take a stroll through Graz, we see green-painted objects on almost every corner—green detailing on benches, green railings, green trash cans, green window shutters. What contributed to the popularity of green metal may very well lie in the famous "Otto Wagner" shade of green, which is everywhere in Vienna. Recently, Wagner's former Suburban and Gürtel line stations underwent renovations and stratigraphic findings showed that the metal surfaces of these stations were originally painted light beige, not the iconic green associated with Wagner. This green coating was applied only after the Second World War. It was commonly used for machine coatings from the 1950s to 1970s. Even the wooden surfaces, now painted green, originally displayed a brown grain pattern.[13] The green of window shutters or other wood elements is a bit harder to explain—country houses in Switzerland were apparently painted green solely to give them a cheerful and pleasant appearance.[14]

Green-stained wood can nevertheless still be found everywhere today, much like green metal surfaces. As already mentioned, coloring wood is no longer life-threatening, so that's one explanation. But why green? One may argue that there is a simple explanation: blending into the greenness of nature, as a sort of subversive greenwashing. Maybe there is an instinct in architects today to shy away, blend in, and pay respects to nature by cosplaying its liveliest, most natural colors, out of shame for building in it at all.

But we believe that architects are, in fact, master tricksters. What is presented as respect and consideration for nature, is actually merely a reinforcement of the building itself. Prematurely—and artificially—patinated, it becomes beautiful and noble, thereby claiming the moral high ground—persistently trying to outsmart its uncertain future.

Sidenote or afterword

The initial form of this text was presented as a public lecture for Diskursiv in January 2023. During the following months after the lecture, many attendees told us that after the lecture, they too were seeing a lot of red and green lately. On that note, we wondered: what came first, and who is perpetuating what?

Notes

1 Espazium, accessed December 15, 2022, https://www.espazium.ch.

2 Paradeigma, Instagram page, accessed December 15, 2022, https://www.instagram.com/paradeigma__/.

3 Otl Aicher and Behnisch & Partner, eds., *On Colour* (Stuttgart: Hatje, 1993), 15.

4 Gordon Shrigley, "Materia 3: Red Oxide," *Drawing Matter*, accessed December 15, 2023, https://drawingmatter.org/materia-3-red-oxide/.

5 Henry Dreyfuss, *Designing for people* (New York: Simon & Schuster, 1955), 192.

6 Kathy Kelleher, "Falu Red, The Color of Bucolic Barns and Mummified Swedes," *The Awl*, accessed December 17, 2022, https://www.theawl.com/2017/12/falu-red-the-color-of-bucolic-barns-and-mummified-swedes/.

7 Ludwig Wappner, Falk Schneemann, and Peter Hoffmann, *Farbige Holzfassaden im urbanen Kontext* (Karlsruhe: KIT, 2022), 50.

8 Stephan Becker, "Béton rouge: Eine kurze Geschichte von Gigon/Guyer bis Pedevilla Architects," *Baunetzwoche#463* (August 2016).

9 Stellwerk Vorbahnhof, Gigon Guyer, accessed January 15, 2023, https://www.gigon-guyer.ch/de/project/stellwerk/.

10 Umbau und Anbau Sammlung Oskar Reinhart "Am Römerholz", Gigon Guyer, accessed January 15, 2023, https://www.gigon-guyer.ch/de/project/sammlung-oskar-reinhart-roemerholz/.

11 Ilka Ruby and Andreas Ruby, eds., *The Materials Book* (Berlin: Ruby Press, 2020), 308.

12 Jan De Vylder, "Talking about Colours" (Diskursiv, Graz, January 24, 2023).

13 Otto-Wagner-Grün: Die Wiener Stadtbahn, Bundesdenkmalamt, accessed December 20, 2022, https://www.bda.gv.at/themen/restaurierwerkstaetten/labor/aktuelle-forschungsergebnisse/otto-wagner-gruen.html.

14 Urs Meier, "Der Fensterladen: Kleines Handbuch zu einem unterschätzten Bauteil," (Berner Fachhochschule Architektur, Holz und Bau, 2018), 8.

Ecologies of Regenerative Color

Paul Konrad

Fig. 1
Bildbauten, Bildbau No. 6, 11, 17, 21, 29, 33,
Montage, Philipp Schaerer, 2009

In the contemporary globalized economy, the color of a building is rarely indicative of the context in which it is situated. While historically, regionally sourced building materials led to distinct local aesthetics, the rise of industrially produced paint has led to a detachment of site, material, and color. All across the globe, thin coats of synthetic resin mixed with pigments get applied to buildings, made up of similar repetitive forms of construction. Regardless of local building tradition and climatic demands, paint has become the one-size-fits-all solution to finishing a building's surface. As the color of façades begin to resemble each other all around the world, one could argue the one thing uniting today's building practice is its indifference to any regional context.

Architects' daily handling of color typically remains on a superficial level. Too often, color is simply treated as a visual characteristic, as a coating without any thickness or particular physical presence. Abbreviated by a short numerical code and accompanied by small printed rectangles, tones and shades are displayed on a standardized chart, so the desired color can be exactly reproduced and later applied to any building component the designer wishes.

One could look at Philipp Schaerer's series of collages, titled *Bildbauten*, as an ironic critique of this phenomenon (Fig. 1). Each collage constructs an image of a fictitious façade. A continuous texture, cropped by a short strip of sky and ground, alludes to the perception of a building without hinting at any tectonic or structural integrity. In this sense, Schaerer constructs the image of a house with a single

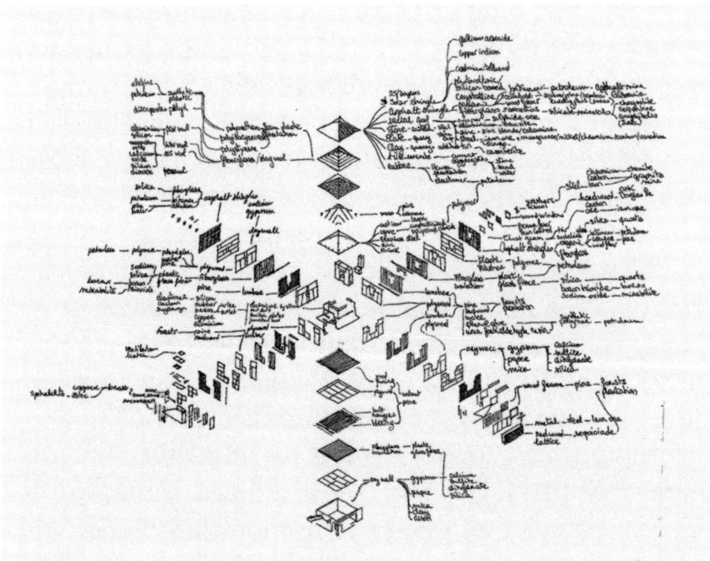

Fig. 2
Scales of Extraction after Morphosis,
Charlotte Malterre-Barthes

two-dimensional texture, mirroring the practice of covering and disguising the labor and material processes that go into a building's production.

All the while, architects tend to neglect the fact that color is also a product of material processes. Be it in the form of paint or as an intrinsic quality of a building material itself, color originates from a process of extracting raw materials.

Most commercially available paint is made up of several key components: pigments, resins, solvents, and additives. Nowadays, the majority of façade paints are either based on minerals like silicate or on the synthetic resins derived from petrochemicals. While these resources are extracted across continents, global supply chains allow them to be processed elsewhere and, ultimately, distributed to sites.

Today's generic use of petrol-based paints is emblematic of what Charlotte Malterre-Barthes calls an architecture of extraction, "a space-making process that requires in its materialization numerous mineral resources acquired via extraction and the reallocation of the Earth's resources."[1] She portrays this expanded view on material processes in her diagram "Scales of Extraction, after Morphosis" (Fig. 2). Here, Barthes traces the path of each building component to its material source in order to highlight the relation between the built environment and complex commodity chains.

The high amount of carbon embodied in matte paint places it as one of the worst performing building materials on a chart measuring global warming potential, which was developed by CINARK, the Center

Fig. 3
The Construction Material Pyramid

for Industrialized Architecture at the Royal Danish Academy (Fig. 3). If we follow the tail of each of these components, we uncover that the designer's choice of a building's color has far wider spatial and societal implications than we usually consider.[2]

Propelled by the urge to increase sustainability in the building sector, one can witness a renewed interest in locally derived colors. For centuries, the colors of vernacular building styles characterized the image of rural settlements. Regional aesthetics were strongly tied to local construction methods. Looking back at historic examples of vernacular architecture one can discover the regenerative potential of colors that are locally sourced.

One of the most iconic regional identities is the red color of Nordic buildings, called *Falun Rød* (falun red). Derived from a locally developed way of processing iron particles into color pigments, it was created to mimic the Central European fixation on copper at the time. Production is still ongoing at the one quarry the color originates from (Fig. 4). But *Falun Rød* also represents a way of enhancing the longevity of local timber façades, protecting them from harsh conditions.

Regional building technologies developed out of a need to work with and engage the immediate surroundings. Materials were sourced locally, distributed in short supply chains, and used in highly performative ways that responded to local climatic and societal demands. The whitewashed buildings found across the Mediterranean, for example, used their highly reflective characteristics to protect

Fig. 4
Falu Gruva: iron-quarry known as the extraction and production site of falun red paint, typical of Swedish timber façades.

settlements from intense radiation and summer heat. As a part of generationally-accumulated knowledge, building practices were strongly tied to local traditions and formed part of a locally derived building culture. Clay-based vernacular architectures can be found across Europe. The Austrian *Weinviertel* clay, for instance, has been pressed into walls and whitewashed with lime or coated with natural paints since the Neolithic era. In Britain meanwhile, local clay was mixed with hay to construct so-called Cob-houses.[3]

While building traditions tend to vary regionally, the composition of building materials also has an enormous effect on regional color schemes. In the process of burning bricks, for example, the ratio of iron and calcium particles, as well as the temperature of burning, determines the color of regional styles. While it might seem obvious to pick a color of brick as an architect, one should be aware of what resources it derives from. Currently, the Austrian federal agency Bundesamt für Geologie funds research projects to discover clay deposits containing low amounts of carbonate. As the type of clay defines how much CO_2 is released during the sintering process, it will also inevitably change the color of bricks.[4] Similarly, common vernacular methods like timber shingles represent a highly ecological mindset, where buildings were constantly repaired and maintained to enhance their lifespan while also continually changing the shade of a façade.

Recently, we have seen a renewed focus on architectural aesthetics shaped by regional material processes. The UK-based NGO "Material Cultures,"

Fig. 5
Stilt House, 2019, Material Cultures

Fig. 6
Stilt House, 2019, Material Cultures

for example, develops prototypes for locally sourced buildings. Together with students, they developed an innovative bio-based demonstrator building called *Stilt House* on the site of an industrial hemp farm (Fig. 5, 6). Besides the low carbon *in situ* hempcrete and spruce stud frame construction, the building's façade is made up of locally sourced hemp fiber cladding. The nut brown color of the corrugated panels stems from a blend of hemp fiber and farm bio-waste resin that mainly consists of corn cob, oat hulls, and bagasse. Like timber, sheets exposed to sunlight will lighten over time. As the buildings mature, so too will the tone of their façades. As such, the house's designers considered the implications of sourcing, producing, and maintaining building materials, while creating an exciting aesthetics of regenerative architecture.

As globalization continues to blur the origins of building materials, it becomes evident that there is a legitimate discussion to be had about the political implications of a building's color. The time has come to rejuvenate a highly ecological building culture, one in which color isn't merely a visual characteristic, but stems from a deep consideration of regenerative material processes.

Notes

1 Charlotte Malterre-Barthes, *Architecture of Extraction: Space and the Political Economy of Construction Materials, Mineral Wealth, and Resource Exhaustion* (2020), accessed 14 May 2023, https://www.charlottemalterrebarthes.com/practice/research-practice/architecture-of-extraction/.

2 See Malterre-Barthes, "The Devil Is in the Details: Who Is It That the World Belongs To?", in *Non-Extractive Architecture: On Designing without Depletion,* ed. Space Caviar (Berlin: Sternberg Press, 2021).

3 See Material Cultures, *Material Reform: Building for a Post-Carbon Future* (London: Mack, 2022), 28–30.

4 Rabeder, J, Lipiarska, I, Reitner, H, Römer A, & Weilbold, *Karbonatarme Tonrohstoffe in Österreich – Bundesweite Übersicht zum Forschungsstand und Charakterisierung der Vorkommen hinsichtlich Rohstoffqualität und -quantität: Bericht über das Arbeitsjahr 2021* (2022), accessed 14 May 2023, https://opac.geologie.ac.at/ais312/detail.aspx.

Interview With Oda Pälmke

Martin Grund
and
Wassily Walter

Fig. 1
Salon Slominski

MG/WW When looking at your work, one gets the impression that there seems to be a recurring palette across projects when it comes to color. Are there colors that you prefer to work with?

OP Yes. I basically only work with two colors from the RAL palette, you can get them at any DIY store: RAL ■■■■ and RAL ■■■■. They are the essence of years of looking at color palettes. I used to call them Prada colors. Today, I no longer explain myself—I would simply consider them "my" colors. You can't immediately recognize them as colors and you often can't tell them apart; depending on the lighting conditions, they more closely resemble the effect of sun and shadow on a used white surface. They are chameleon colors—they are constantly changing, they are ever new, they are my preferred, absolutely timeless material.

MG/WW It sounds like "color" in the true sense of the word is not particularly important to you.

OP As an architect, I mainly work with the mediums of space and form. If I had to choose between color and form, I wouldn't have to think about it at all. I'm interested in the form. The space is the setting and framing. Color is created through its use. For the renovation I did on Simon Fujiwara and Ingar Dragset's apartment, for example, they wanted to paint every room in a very strong color, Schinkelesque. I considered this interesting because it was unnecessary, since there were already huge, colorful

Fig. 2
Secret Library

tiled stoves in these rooms, which gave each room its own color. So, the whole apartment was painted white-gray, RAL ■■■■. When you walk through the rooms, one room appears blue, another gold and another red, depending on which stove is currently in it.

MG/WW Does that mean those colors that go beyond RAL ■■■■ and RAL ■■■■—and this occurs quite frequently in your projects—are determined by the client?

OP When people ask me for colors, I often see it as a kind of service. But with artists, it's always enriching and surprising. In fact, I don't feel like I use that many colors. I'd rather use mirrors in a space—they double the sense of life and life is known to be colorful. The space is just the background for the staging of life.

MG/WW What is your intention behind it?

OP I would say that I aspire to design and build spaces that look as if they have always been there. Spaces that don't give you the idea that they were designed in a contemporary way. Of course, I don't mean anything historicizing by this—that a room has to have stucco, for instance, or a façade needs plinths and parapets. That doesn't interest me at all. I'm interested in a timeless space that you find pleasant, where it becomes hard to tell whether it was just designed by me or has always been like this. As an

Fig. 3
Pumpwerk/Pumping station

architect, why do I have to paint yellowed door frames when I can also declare the old white to be the new white. It works just as well with other colors. Take Beate Slominski's salon in Berlin-Wilmersdorf, which is the same oak-paneled room in which Nicolaus Sombart held his Sunday salons. The room was painted a dark green, which was really dominant. I wanted to free Beate from it without eliminating the story, so I designed a weave, a structure in the bright colors of her furniture (which already existed and which I didn't have to design), and declared the green to be the background. The complex color scheme actually evolved this way—you could call it coincidence or an act of providence. On reflection, this conceptual approach of allowing for coincidence is of course a confrontation with Hermann Czech and also a longing for self-evidence.

MG/WW How can we envisage your collaboration with artists?

OP It varies. I really work a lot for (and therefore also *with*) artists when they commission me as an architect. If there is a desire for color, I don't feel like I have to explain to an artist what good colors are. I respond to individual ideas and use them conceptually, but I always combine them with my colors, which frames them in a particular way. So, anything is possible.

I am good friends with the Icelandic artist Gudny Gudmundsdottir—we worked together on the Secret Library for Jonathan Meese, for example.

Fig. 4
The Post Republic

My design is a fictionalized principle of order for the rooms, with closed bookshelves on all the walls. The rhombic structure results from geometric rules, so everything can be explained logically. Milling rhomboids into MDF paneling doesn't cost any money, so they were built from the simplest of materials; actually just from standard building components that were precisely designed, lined up, and joined to create a poetically-charged whole. That would have been enough for me, I could have sufficed with two colors.

In the collaboration with Gudny, the entire architectural construction then became the background, the painting ground for around fifty shades of NCS blue, which were applied with a roller. Gudny determined the colors; during our conversations, which were characterized by total trust, there was always a picture of Whistler and Jeckyll's famous Peacock Room on the table. At the same time, it was clear that it would be a light blue and a light green, because the rooms were to reflect an Icelandic ice cave: an igloo and an ivy-covered dacha in summer, ideal quiet rooms for a secret library. In this respect, the colors here also have a conceptual meaning. To some extent, the artist has followed the architect's order, to some extent she has resisted it. The colors always change with the milling of the rhomboids, but in one of the rooms Gudny has introduced a yellow that does not exist elsewhere. This yellow is the only moment where two colors are next to each other on one level. I found it too playful, but for that very reason fascinating and inexplicable. So, one room has become the artist's room and the other the architect's room.

It is the interplay of "The Logic and the Magic": a room like a peacock's feather—you can choose any color you want and it will be beautiful anyway because the form is right. That's my second thesis: form is more important than color.

MG/WW And you're not necessarily only talking about a preference for spatial, but also two-dimensional form, right? Geometric shapes and patterns, structures are a recurring theme, both in your drawings and in your built spaces.

OP I use a pattern, or rather a structure—a system, a dimensional regulator—in existing situations that I rearrange geometrically without having to make major structural changes. I introduced ceiling painting in the library of Jonathan Meese's pumping station. Here, I used the rhombic pattern to geometrically straighten the relatively lopsided room, so to speak. The geometric structure is aligned in such a way that it fits perfectly. Every point, every corner fits. But the impression is deceptive: it's just not right, or rather it's not the even, parallel, "correct" geometry that you would expect at first glance. But the eye doesn't notice this and the room looks right. The rhombic pattern is the fictionalization of the ideal space, which arises in perception and does not have to be materialized. Fictionalization instead of replacing materialization. Incidentally, this is also a sustainable design method. The respective colors of these patterns are also selected on the basis of conceptual considerations. With Gudny Gudmundsdottir,

I once chose RAL 1000 as the color for a project. This is "green-beige," the first and—as we found—the poorest of all RAL colors by name. We wanted to make the color chic. I then had number 1000 mixed at the hardware store for a test and it really was the case that no one had ever ordered this color before. I was very pleased with the concept of declaring the most modest solution as sexy. You can apply this to many materials.

MG/WW Speaking of material, what is your relationship to it?

OP I really design almost everything with color (here I mean color, the material). I used to think that an architecture office definitely had a collection of materials, the more extensive the better. But that only ever exhausted me. I'm not interested in materials above a minimum level, let alone multi-layered components. I'm very happy when I can cover heterogeneous materials and shapes with RAL ■■■■ and RAL ■■■■.

MG/WW Does that also apply to the house on Beuthstrasse—a newly designed urban building block?

OP In principle, the same rules apply inside and out. The Beuthstrasse apartment building is a building with an ETICS façade for a large Berlin project development company. I tried to look at it as an academic project. I thought, if I'm really involved in the construction of a thermal skin façade, then I shouldn't do anything pseudo-tectonic here with a difficult material. Instead, I tried to cultivate a modest, clean 50/60s reconstruction expression and design a structure, a fabric, a garment for the building. It was not at all easy to achieve this total reduction, the image of economy and banality. The blue foyer in the building was actually created by economizing. I wanted to bring the brick inside the building, but that was cut in a construction meeting. They said: "Ms. Pälmke, why don't you choose a nice color?" I then chose a beautiful (!) blue—a quote from the blue façade on the courtyard side of a social housing development in Wedding, Drontheimer Strasse, which I had planned in 1990–96 when I was a project manager in the Kollhoff Timmermann office. Back then, we called it "expressive after-work blue," so it was already a conceptually chosen color; in the foyer of Beuthstrasse, it is applied as a quote that is doubly conceptual, if you can put it that way.

MG/WW Is there a similar story behind the project for The Post Republic, an ideal cinema for film post-production?

OP This project in the 2010s was in part a freestanding new build, as an extension to a car sales hall erected without planning permission in the still-empty, reunified Berlin. A fence had to be built around the site at the time: private property—no trespassing. Nowadays, the building is completely enclosed. As an architect, I could have done something contemporary and beautiful using a great, trendy material, perhaps a chic colored concrete or something like that. I didn't do that and I still think that's exactly right today. The ensemble of buildings looks as if it has always been there. In the 1990s, there were these car sales halls everywhere and they reminded me a bit of the circus in Wim Wenders's film *Wings of Desire* (1987). Back then, we wanted to preserve this poor, wild time of the 2000s, leaving these halls as they were and continuing to build them in the same vulgar way. The most interesting people are always in the places where there is basically nothing. Florian Heilmeyer once called it "[t]he invisible architecture of OP" and, looking back, I realize this more and more. I have an old photo book about Berlin here in the studio, with lots of aerial photos of the city. They are all color photographs, somewhere on the spectrum between light beige and light gray: Berlin Colors, Poor colors, Background.

The Color of the Architectural Skin

Matthias Castorph

Like every body, the architectural body also requires a skin. At the interface between the building structure and the exterior space, a (more or less) thick layer is formed that encloses the body and creates the visible surface. This color of the skin, as the thinnest layer known to architecture, essentially determines the setting. Through its color, the skin ultimately defines the appearance as well as the collective image of the architectural body—after all, it is impossible to overlook color.

As the surface, the skin is more sensitive than the actual body, since it is most directly exposed to environmental influences. It must be constantly cared for, repaired if damaged, and renewed again and again over the years. In the case of historically relevant bodies, this renewal becomes a problem that is inversely proportional to the thinness of the component, as the skin (and thus the appearance of heritage) is not just about the care of the skin, but also about the preservation of heritage as a cultural task. Questions therefore arise as to how this final layer, which significantly determines the reading and perception of architectural bodies, can be captured—what shade of color, what purity, what brightness is therefore right?

As with other issues surrounding the preservation of built heritage, it is worth looking back to one of the original texts of heritage preservation, *The Venice Charter*, which was declared in 1964. The charter demands that architectural heritage should be "handed on in the full richness of [its] authenticity," its legacy transmitting an intellectual message. The aim of all conservation, renovation, and restoration is thus to both preserve and maintain the historical testimony. Article 7 continues: "The monument is inseparable from the history to which it bears witness."

But what does this mean in concrete terms? What does it mean for your own practice? An example: the renovation of a post office building, the so-called "Goethepost," which we recently carried out with our office, was a listed icon of modern architecture in Munich. Planned and realized between 1927 and 1932, it was assembled according to the designs by architects Walther Schmidt and Franz Holzhammer, under the direction of Robert Vorhoelzer, as protagonists of the Postbauschule. Designed in the New Objectivity style, it is one of the few representatives of "White Modernism" in Munich. The elegant, curved five-story building, structured by ribbon windows and window squares, is characterized by its pure, smooth, light-colored skin. In historical black and white images, it stands out strikingly from the gray of the surrounding city (Fig. 1). So, how do you deal with the skin during renovation? What color should the building be given?

From today's perspective, this particular example of "New Objectivity," with its light-colored paint, is in line with "White Modernism" as we know it from the Bauhaus or Le Corbusier's surviving pictures. Here, the smooth, light skin stands for purity, clarity, and the renunciation of color. It is an attempt to radically dispose of the meanings conveyed by pre-modernist façades, with their emphasis on the architecture's surface. In the images of architectural propaganda of that time, the white of the "bodies" forms a strong

Fig. 1
Post office at Goetheplatz
in Munich, 1932

contrast with the black of the openings and shadows, creating an almost sculptural effect: images of "either/or" in black or white, preferably without any nuances in between.

We now know from scientific studies that, analogous to the myth that ancient temples—whose purity and clarity Johann Joachim Winckelmann glorified in the eighteenth century—were colorless (when they were in fact brightly painted), "White Modernism" was not really white at all. Rather, it alternated between white, gray, and beige. Color—and even gilding—certainly had its place, for example in the modernist holy of holies, namely the Bauhaus master houses in Dessau. Modernism was therefore not quite as white as we have been led to believe.

As an abstract "truth," this contradiction between knowledge and belief about the supposed "whiteness" of modernity's skin does not affect us as long as it does not impact us personally. But what happens when it becomes concrete?

During the survey of the existing post office building, it turned out that the building was originally beige, almost light brown—not white, as it had been known in the cityscape for over seventy years and as it had been stored in the collective imaginary. It was discovered that, after the war damage had been repaired, layer after layer of white had been applied over the original first coat (Fig. 2). What to do? How to decide between the historical authenticity of the building component and the authenticity of the collective image that history had created in the meantime?

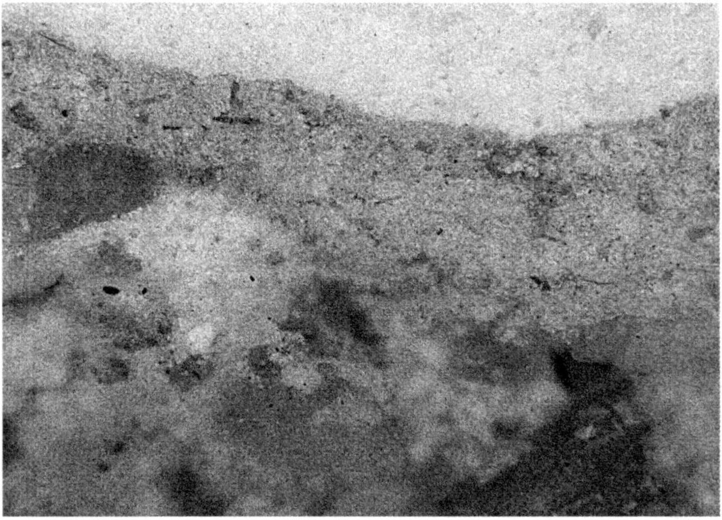

Fig. 2
Findings: Cross-section sample façade surface (50× magnification)

Looking back again at *The Venice Charter*: if one takes seriously the notion that monuments should convey an intellectual message through the richness of their authenticity, then this also means that the connection between the concrete reality of a building component and the architecture of the building (in the context of its history) cannot be abandoned. Thus, on the one hand, the concrete coloring of the original state, as well as the entire construction history of the architectural object, belong to the building. On the other hand, authenticity includes not only the scientifically substantiated history of the object, but also the stories associated with it, namely all the collective images, experiences, and myths that have formed since its construction—architectural components as visible elements, understood as carriers of history and stories.

Intellectually, the question of authenticity in the choice of color can not simply be resolved in the abstract. In practice, however, you have to make a concrete decision—either/or—since there is only one color for a house. Do you follow the conviction that you are choosing the original color that has been found, in other words the historically "correct" one? Or do you opt for the version that is correct in terms of meaning? Do you stay with the original color, or do you preserve the collective memory?

We have decided in favor of white. The colorless image remains.

Afterword, Biographies, Contributions Index, Exhibition

Afterword
Julian Brües

After building models, we wanted to tackle another topic that has been pushed into the background, and so, *"Blauäugig und grün hinter den Ohren,"*[1] we ventured into the topic of color in architecture. With the exhibition of the same name, in which ninety international offices took part, we gained an overview of the significance of color in today's architectural world. These images—of buildings, drawings, and simply captured architectural moments—also provide a framework for this publication and the wider reflection it encourages: for noting, reading, and thinking about theoretical discourses and points of view.

The twenty contributions included here represent the diversity that color can bring to our everyday built environment. The book is by no means intended to be a manifesto for color, but rather a stimulus or impetus for readers to think again about color—its use and its radiance.

How can a book on such a subjective topic possibly be evaluated? Aren't there more important design decisions than the color of bathroom tiles? We're not interested in making designs, architecture, or buildings more colorful. Rather, this book should simply provoke a conservation about the current treatment of this dry topic.

Essentially, it's about how architects, students of architecture, and those who enjoy architecture perceive things—how they see them, understand them, interpret them, and remember them.

Colors are usually in the background. They tend to convey meaning subconsciously. When we think of a city, do we think of its color? Is there such a thing as the color of a city? The old town, downtown, the suburbs? Or is it layers of time we think of? The nostalgic, the coolly reflective (progressive), and the attention-seeking?

Ultimately, I found myself having to decide on a color for an exhibition display. I pulled out a color fan, combined the "best" three shades of blue, photographed them and wrote down the identification. Already, I began to doubt myself. I returned to the color fan, selected some other shades of blue. I photographed these and wrote them down again.

There are too many shades of blue—this is a good thing. I made a sample, cut the beech wood to size, had the glaze made up at the DIY store, and used the brush myself. I left it to dry and applied a second glaze to half of the three samples. I held a color fan up to it and compared it with the other shades in the exhibition.

One it is—decision made. I wrote an e-mail and sent it off. The sample from the painting company arrived and, again, I was filled with uncertainty. Is it really this color? I sought reassurance from a colleague. The painter called and approved my choice.

Where does this uncertainty come from? We studied color theory at university. There are also plenty of books and websites we can draw from to create the perfect color combinations and have them made up.

In summary, it can be said that looking at color was a very informative undertaking. It's often used to give a building, room, or architecture a quick "kick," infusing it with some excitement.

But color is much more than this: it creates identification. It generates depth. It has an unexpected honesty. It plays nimbly with appearances. It focuses and emphasizes. It distracts and disguises. It is a fascinating tool.

That is why this book pleads for a deeper, more joyful examination of the subject that surrounds us every day: color. We would like to thank our co-authors for their trust and their invaluable contributions, as well as the many other people who made this book possible. We are incredibly proud of it.

Notes

1 "*Blauäugig*" (blue-eyed) and "*grün hinter den Ohren*" (green behind the ears) are two German expressions, which translate to "half-baked" or "to be wet behind the ears."

Adna Babahmetović, born in Bosnia and Herzegovina, studied architecture at TU Graz where she focused on the topics of housing and memory under Prof. Alex Lehnerer. During and after her studies she worked for various architecture offices, including SLETH Architects in Aarhus and Schenker Salvi Weber Architekten in Vienna. She is currently based in Vienna, where she works as a university assistant at the Research Unit of Housing and Design at TU Vienna. She is a part of Diskursiv and together with her twin sister, Ajna, she co-founded the studio "Ajna i Adna," which focuses on competitions and other forms of architectural production.

Ajna Babahmetović, born in Bosnia and Herzegovina, studied architecture at TU Graz. Her master's thesis investigated spatial manifestations of migration in Bosnia and Herzegovina, its results have been published and presented in Graz, Berlin, and Sarajevo. She has written for *Failed Architecture*, *Drawing Matter*, *GAM*, and *Kolik Film Magazine*. Ajna has worked for various architecture offices, including Riegler Riewe Architects and Atelier Frühwirth. Currently, she works as a teaching and research associate at the KOEN Institute at TU Graz. She is a part of Diskursiv and together with her twin sister, Adna, she co-founded the studio "Ajna i Adna," which focuses on competitions and other forms of architectural production.

Alexander Barina is an architect and guest lecturer at the Berlin University of the Arts. After studying at the Bauhaus-Universität Weimar, the UdK Berlin, and ETH Zurich, he worked with Meier Hug Architekten in Zurich, Adolf Krischanitz in Vienna, and Lacaton & Vassal in Paris. Since 2018, he has been working firstly at TU Wien and then with Anne Femmer and Florian Summa at TU Graz. Until 2020, he curated the architecture blog TÉCHNE: Architectural Juxtaposition.

Julian Brües is an architect. He graduated from TU Graz (Austria) with a BSc and from the ZHAW (Switzerland) with an MA. He has worked for offices such as Lederer Ragnarsdóttir Oei (Stuttgart) and Furrer Jud (Zurich). Since March 2020 he has been working as a university assistant at the Institut Raum und Gestalt. His research and teaching focuses on is the "fragmented figure" in the field of structure and expression. In 2020, he received the Start Scholarship for Architecture and Design, which he used to found Diskursiv, an association for architectural research.

Francesco Caneschi was born in Florence. His PhD project, financed by FCT and developed at FAUP (Porto, PT) and at DIDA (Florence, IT), is entitled: "Glocal Tools: Temporary urban actions for collective production of space." He has worked for the University of Aveiro (PT), for Aires Mateus Associados (Lisbon, PT), and for Orizzontale (Rome, IT). He is the co-founder of Alibi. His research interests are in radical architecture and incremental urbanism.

Matthias Castorph is an architect and urban planner. He studied architecture at TU Munich with Friedrich Kurrent and Uwe Kiessler. He was an assistant to Andreas Hild and received his PhD from TU Kaiserslautern in 1999. After his junior professorship at the TU Kaiserslautern (2002–2008), he taught as a visiting professor at the TU Munich and as an adjunct professor at the TU Kaiserslautern, where he represented the teaching and research area "Stadtbaukunst." He was appointed university professor in 2020. In 2021, he became head of the Institute of Design in Existing Structures and Architectural Heritage Protection at TU Graz. Together with his partners Felicia Lehmann and Haiko Tabillion, he co-founded the architecture practice Lehmann, Tabillion & Castorph Architektur Stadtplanung Gesellschaft mbH in Munich (until December 2021 Goetz Castorph Architekten und Stadtplaner GmbH). Together with his team, Matthias Castorph is involved in urban planning, development consulting for municipalities, the design and realization of new buildings (with a focus on residential and office buildings), buildings in existing structures, and renovations in accordance with heritage protection.

Jan Engelke lives in Berlin and works and researches with the collaborative architecture practice ANA on publications, architecture, and exhibition projects. After studying architecture in Zurich and Weimar, he completed a doctoral project at TU Munich "Die eigenen vier Wände," on the home of one's own in post-war West Germany and the magazine *Schöner*

Wohnen. Most recently, he published *Offenbach Kaleidoskop* (Spector Books 2022).

Martin Grund is a German architect who currently lives in Basel. After his studies in Cottbus and Mendrisio, and internships in Basel, Zurich, and Berlin, he gained his first work experience at the Basel architecture firm jessenvollenweider. He is currently working with the young Basel office Kooperative E45.

Michael Hafner is an architect in Vienna and Porto. He studied at the TU Graz and at the Faculdade de Arquitetura da Universidade do Porto. After graduating, he worked in various architectural offices in Austria, such as ARTEC Architekten. Since 2022, he has been teaching and researching at the Institut für Entwerfen im Bestand und Denkmalpflege at TU Graz. Alongside this, he has been working with Katharina Hohenwarter as Studio Bonfim since 2019. He became a member of the association for architectural research Diskursiv in 2021 and was awarded with the Start Scholarship for Architecture and Design in 2023.

Franziska Hederer studied architecture in Austria and the Netherlands and is associate professor at the Institute Raum und Gestalt at TU Graz. In 2015, with her work "At the Oscillating Margins of Architecture," she habilitated in the field of spatial perception and experimental design. She has taught and lectured at TU Liverpool, University of Antwerp, KTH Stockholm, University of Madeira, and University of Applied Arts in Vienna.

Nikola Hergovich studied architecture at TU Vienna. He has worked in architectural offices, at the institute Raumgestaltung und Entwerfen and as an assistant for photographers and artists. He is a self-taught photographer and transdisciplinary artist. His artistic work is a blend of different interests and disciplines—often but not only operating in the field of architecture. Since 2014, he is represented in various exhibitions and publications. In 2023, he released a photo book about anonymous architecture titled *Naive Architektur*. He lives and works in Vienna.

Katharina Hohenwarter is an architect in Vienna and Porto. She studied at TU Graz and undertook a research stay at the Faculdade de Arquitetura da Universidade do Porto. After graduating, she worked with Claudia Cavallar, among others, and held teaching positions at TU Vienna—at the Institut für Gestaltungslehre and the Institut für Gebäudelehre. Since 2019, Hohenwarter has been working with Michael Hafner under the name Studio Bonfim and since 2023 as a university assistant at TU Graz, alongside the Chair of Integral Architecture, Prof. Lisa Yamaguchi. In 2021, she became a member of the association for architectural research, Diskursiv.

HPO is an emerging community of eleven architects based in Ferrara, Italy. Formed in 2017 to escape the university routine and face the challenges of the job market, HPO has been working on temporary installations, exhibitions, events, and performances, always maintaining a collaborative attitude. HPO HQ is the group's headquarters in Ferrara, from which it operates as part of a hyper-connected province, a rooting that has nonetheless led the group to exhibit its work at some of Europe's leading design centers and universities: Akademie der Künste, Berlin, HEAD, Geneva, TU Graz, ENSAP Versailles, and Dropcity, Milan.

Institut Vierzehn was founded in the summer of 2022 and is a student collective spanning the fields of architecture, art, urban planning, and crafts. It is not based on individual persons, but sees itself as a space for the joint development of topics. They are dedicated to current issues in architecture and see themselves as a complement to the student discourse in Graz. They do not claim to have comprehensive, complete knowledge as a basis. They develop through trial and error, experimentation and free creation, relying on the accumulated (half-)knowledge of students. The exchange takes place at the Institut Vierzehn in the form of workshops, exhibitions, lectures, and discussions. The aim is to teach and learn what is not taught, and to pay attention to what is not observed.

Paul Konrad is an architect with a focus on wider urban and societal issues. During his time at the the Royal Danish Academy in Copenhagen and the TU Graz he gained an educational background in the architectural, as well as the strategic and research-based urban scale. Paul worked for several offices in Berlin, Vienna, and Copenhagen. His current work at Atelier Loidl centers on an urban strategy for the resilient future of a flood prone area of the Ahrtal, combining climate adaptations strategies with the restoration of civic infrastructures.

Alex Lehnerer is an architect and teacher. Before his appointment as professor in Graz, he was assistant professor at the ETH Zurich and at the School of Architecture in Chicago. He designed the German Pavilion in Venice in 2014; his books include *Grand Urban Rules* (NAi010 2009/2014), *The Western Town* (Hatje Cantz, 2013), and *Bungalow Germania* (Hatje Cantz, 2014). He holds a PhD from the ETH Zurich, a master's degree from UCLA, and a diploma from the TU Berlin. His architectural office is located in Zurich and Erlangen.

Elise Limon is an architectural designer, researcher and writer currently based in New Haven. She holds a BA in Architecture from the University of Cambridge and an M.Arch II from the post-professional programme at Yale University. She enjoys and actively seeks out collaboration. She is interested in the future of landscapes, ecosystems, and the entanglements of architecture with extractive materials and economic logics. Her writing has appeared in *The Architectural Review*, *Paprika!* and *trans magazine*, ETH. She is currently co-editing a book on law and public space.

Tabea Marschall is an artist, curator, and writer based in Berlin. She studied Fine Arts at the University of the Arts Berlin under Monica Bonvicini and received her MA from the postgraduate programme in Critical Studies at the Academy of Fine Arts Vienna. Her work revolves around feminist practices of writing (in) oneself, as performative inscriptions and polyphonic modes of writing. She questions the legibility and materiality of this writing, which cannot be conceived without its own situatedness in language and can be read as a polyphony working together. Her writing has appeared in various publications of the Academy of Fine Arts and the University of the Arts. She regularly publishes exhibition reviews in various magazines such as *PW Magazine*, *Monopol*, and *von hundert*.

Marina Montresor studied architecture at the Accademia di Architettura in Mendrisio. She has worked for Christian Kerez, Zurich, and Made In, Geneva, and has collaborated with the magazine *Domus* in Milano. Together with Stephan Lando, Marina has published *Defining Criteria* (Quart Verlag, 2018) and in 2019 started the office Gradient. Since 2018 she has been involved in teaching and research within the Chair of Architectural Design Charbonnet-Heiz at the ETH Zurich, where she is responsible for the master's thesis. In 2020, Marina started her PhD investigating verticality in Los Angeles, supervised by Prof. François Charbonnet.

Julian Müller is a sociologist. He currently is visiting professor at TU Graz, where he teaches courses on urban and architectural ethnography. He was deputy professor at the University of Marburg, assistant professor at the University of Munich and also worked, among other places, at the University of Lucerne, the Keio University Tokyo, and the Bavarian Academy of Sciences and Humanities. Together with Matthias Castorph he founded the "Institut für Allgemeinarchitektur," based in Munich, which investigates urban banality, ordinary architecture, and everyday situations.

Adam Sherman is a research associate with the research unit of Gestaltungslehre und Entwerfen at TU Vienna. His writings and design projects have been featured in various publications and institutions, most recently in the *ACADIA Journal* and at the CICA Museum in Seoul. He has practiced with a number of internationally recognized firms, including SO – IL and OMA, and studied architecture at Harvard University and structural engineering at Columbia University.

Rafał Śliwa is an architect and co-curator of the *Trouble in Paradise* exhibition in the Polish Pavilion at the 17th International Architecture Exhibition – La Biennale di Venezia. He is co-founder of PROLOG and currently practices at Christian Kerez Office in Milan. He studied architecture in Portugal and Poland, at the University of Minho in Guimarães, the University of Coimbra, and the University of Porto. He completed his master's thesis at the Wrocław University of Technology, investigating the relationship between the architecture of the city and education. He has worked for offices in Poland and Portugal on competitions and concept designs.

Philipp Sternath is a cultural economist, who earned his bachelor's degree in economics from the Karl-Franzens University (Austria) and a master's of Arts & Culture from the Erasmus University Rotterdam (Netherlands). His research focuses on the creative industries, with a specific interest in the architectural sector. He is founding member of the association Diskursiv, that explores the cultural tensions in this field of practice and tries to expose them through exhibitions as well as publications.

Luca Tommasi is a PhD holder and licensed architect. A former teaching assistant at Politecnico di Bari from 2016 to 2022, he has been a guest lecturer and researcher at the TU Eindhoven, in the "Rational architecture" research group led by Christian Rapp between 2020 and 2021. He is regularly invited to international workshops and exhibitions, and currently lives and works in Bari.

Wassily Walter is an architect and teacher based between Berlin and Vienna. In parallel to projects operating across various scales, he has been collaborating with the architecture office Kuehn Malvezzi since 2019. Here, he was involved in a number of international cultural projects such as the interreligious initiative House of One in Berlin and the conversion of Batiment d'Art Contemporain in Geneva. Since 2021 he has been teaching at the Chairs of Wilfried Kuehn and Pier Paolo Tamburelli at TU Vienna and as workshop tutor at the University and the Royal Academy of Fine Arts in Antwerp.

wohnlabor is a collective Anna Jäger and Rebekka Hirschberg founded together with three colleagues in 2018. Anna works as an architect in Graz, while Rebekka is pursuing a PhD in urbanism in Ghent and Vienna. The wohnlabor collective is dedicated to exploring housing as a critical component of urban development, focusing on architectural design, communal living, social sustainability, and ecological impact. Through publications, exhibitions, and public events, wohnlabor contributes to the discourse on how to create urban environments that meet society's diverse needs.

Max Otto Zitzelsberger graduated from the TU Munich in 2009. After undertaking freelance work in various architecture offices in Germany and Switzerland, he held a position in the Academic Council at the Chair of Prof. Florian Nagler, "Design and Construction," at the TU Munich from 2010 to 2017. Zitzelsberger has been working on own projects since 2011, for which he was awarded the Weissenhof Architecture Prize in 2018 and also received a Scholarship of German Academy Rome in 2019. In the same year, he took up a junior professorship at the TU Kaiserslautern, which he currently holds. In 2023, he was part of the exhibition in the German Pavilion at the Venice Architecture Biennale with students from TU Kaiserslautern.

A Gesture Of is a design studio that supports institutions, organizations, and individuals in translating their values into holistic visual systems for campaigns, digital products, and more.

Contributions
Index #–Z

① Favorite color
② Favorite surface
③ Favorite technique
④ Favorite colorful house

31/44 Architects
① For inclusion in a new building it would most likely be something you could already find very nearby... ② Materials which have color within and throughout them, not just on their surface ③ Color comes from the surroundings and prevailing traditions; we find them rather than propose them ④ Ca d'Oro, Venice. The colored stones are still beautiful, imagine when it was also decorated with gold ...

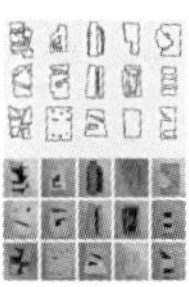

ANAH
① Color of the earth, soil in campos ② Exposed concrete ③ Pigmented concrete ④ James King House, Paulo Mendes da Rocha, 1972

architecture uncomfortable workshop
① Dark yellow ② Beeswax ③ Beeswax pouring and patching ④ Beehouse

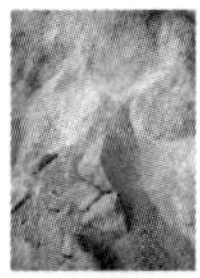

ARHIV architecture & urbanism
① The gradient between light blue and yellow during dawn and how it reflects back onto the surroundings ② The sheen of polished but matte stone finish ③ Back when it was possible, electro-galvanizing metal to have a rainbow patina ④ Can't decide between Casa Malaparte by Adalberto Libera or Can Lis by Jørn Utzon. Both different examples on how to make mediterranean but cinematic houses

Atelier Amont
① Electric ② Rough ③ Glaze ④ Chehel Sotoun

ATELIERDACOSTA
① Can't say favorite colors, only color combinations, e.g., plain red, blue, green, yellow with raw textured materials ② Wood, even if always afraid to be more beautiful if left raw. ③ Brushes, for the reason given above. With aqueous paint you still get the raw texture beneath ④ Brummel House, Adolf Loos

Atelier do Corvo
① Blue ② Wood ③ Craft ④ Casa Malaparte, Adalberto Libera

Atelier Starzak Strebicki
① RAL 6019 ② Wood ③ HPL plywood and stained wood ④ Interiors designed by Charlotte Perriand and Gio Ponti

Atelier van Berlo
① C:0% M:74% Y:86% K:0% ② Terrazzo ③ Bricolage ④ La Muralla Roja, Ricardo Bofill

BATIMENTS
① NCS S 1015-R10B ② XPS ③ Spray Paint ④ Office for Famous Agency, Groot-Bijgaarden, BE Architecten De Vylder Vinck Taillieu

BELT
① Antwerp Blue, C1 M40 Y30 K10 ② Wood, steel, and tile surfaces ③ Researching color combinations from favorite paintings or from the book *A Dictionary Of Color Combinations* ④ Looshaus am Kreuzberg vormals Landhaus Khuner, Adolf Loos

Bovenbouw Architectuur
① Difficult to answer this question. Colors depend on settings. In general we like complex colors, which are hard to give a simple name to.There are a few colors that return often in our practice. RAL 90 is a grayish white that performs well as an outdoor white. In heritage projects we like to use S-1002-y as a light gray for doors or skirtings that contrast nicely with a white wall. ② Most certainly one cannot make a colorful interior that relies too much on paint. If you want to mix many colors in one space, most colors need to be embedded, otherwise the space will feel shallow and artificial. Staining wood can be challenging, but has great potential to accentuate and color the grain of the wood in a single gesture. ③ Coolors is a website we use regularly. It allows you to speed up the potential of unpredictable colors in a space or in a series of spaces. I feel it never offers the solution, but it does catalyze the discussion around color options. ④ This is the Faaborg Museum by Carl Petersen. It is a small museum made up of a beautiful *enfilade* of rooms. It is very colorful. There is a wonderful color sequence with a blue octagon, a large red room, and a series of small yellow rooms. None of the colors are too straightforward, and the combinations add to the general idea of the building.

Bruncken Frett Architekten
① Rosa ② Douglasien Holz ③ Abstraktion ④ Enrico Fermi School Turin. BDR bureau

BUERO41A
① According to the space, materiality and idea—and blue ② According to the space, materiality and idea—and blue ③ According to the space, materiality and idea—and blue ④ De Vylder Vinck Taillieu—Scheeplos

BUREAU
① Wong Kar-Wai's *Ashes of Time* ② The earth's as it is in *The Gaia Paradigm* ③ Janet Sobel's all-over painting technique ④ Schrõder House, Gerrit Rietveld, 1924

CABINET
① Blue ② Any expressive texture: plywood e.g. ③ Oil glaze (water thinnable), three coats, twenty-four-hour interval per coat
④ Refurbishment of Nuora House, Alvar Aalto (Jyväskylä, Finland)

CHYBIK + KRISTOF
① Red ② Honest and natural
③ Experimental ④ Cuadra San Cristóbal by Luis Barragán, Lorenzo Zandri

Cierto Estudio
① So many... couldn't say just one! ② Natural materials: marble, wood... ③ Micro-cement ④ Walden 7, Ricardo Bofill

coabitare
① NCS S 1010-B10G
② Concrete formwork panel
③ Brushstroke ④ Kaiserjosef-platz 4, 8010 Graz

COCI
① Pink ② Screen ③ White lines and solid colors ④ Nadja, Point Supreme

COMTE/MEUWLY
① 05:13 ② 13:27 ③ 23:30
④ 19:42

Corpo Atelier
① Pearl White ② Stone(s)
③ Plaster ④ Smiljan Radic, La Habitación, Chiloé Island

CORREIA/RAGAZZI ARQUITECTOS
① / ② / ③ / ④ /

Čović + Köroğlu
① Blue ② Comb finish ③ Broom finish ④ La Muralla Roja

Demo Working Group
① Nude ② Anodized ③ Powder coated ④ Hochschule für Musik und Tanz, Köln

Detour Universe
① Verde mare, panda edition
② Wood Veneer Alpi Makassar 911 ③ Marbleizing ④ Kazunari Sakamoto: Machiya hiouse, Daita, 1970

draftworks* architects
① Terracotta ② Concrete
③ Geometric painting
④ Walden 7, Ricardo Bofill

Eagles of Architecture
① Hunter green ② Pitch Pine and Gypsum Board Panel
③ Pure material, no technique
④ Construction sites, New York

EBBA
① Signal Orange ② Clay
③ Venetian plaster ④ La Muralla Roja by Ricardo Bofill

Enrique Espinosa (Eeestudio) / Lys Villalba
① Green/yellow ② Raw ones/undulated ones ③ Reuse / Material Crossovers ④ Latapie House, Lacaton Vassal; La Muralla Roja, Ricardo Bofill

EHRL BIELICKY
① Cadium red light ② Sealed/lacquered raw wood/metal
③ Galvanized, hammered
④ House VI, Peter Eisenman

fabulism
① Blue ② Water ③ Collage
④ Jardin Majorelle

fala
① A blue that feels green to some, somewhere around ral5020. ② Marble ③ Collage
④ House like a die, by Takefumi Aida

False Mirror Office
① Neon pink ② Gold foil
③ Collage ④ Sammezzano's Castle

David Fink, Lukas Fink, Tobias Fink
① The color that adds a new fresh layer ② The surface which is already there ③ The most pragmatic technique for the respective situations
④ One of many: Umlauftank by Ludwig Leo

Franziska Singer Architektur
① Dark blue ② Wood ③ Paint/ Laquer ④ E.1027, Eileen Gray

GANG Atelier
① lightpink-green ② All by Hermann Czech ③ Eye-dropper ④ Meisterhaus Kandinsky/ Klee

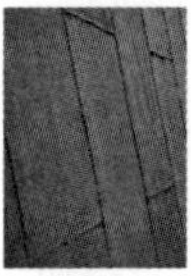

GIPP arkitektur
① Black ② Tar paper
③ Gluing ④ Bruder Klaus Field Chapel

Groothuijse de Boer architecten
① Soft green ② Coarse plaster
③ Pigmenting ④ Villa Snellman, Erik Gunnar Asplund (1917)

GROSZSTADT
① 8d4666 ② Wallpaper
③ Digital Print ④ Greek temple

Habsburg Isele Architekten
① Old Plum Jam ② Solid wood ③ Anodized ④ Carlo Scarpa, Villa Ottolenghi

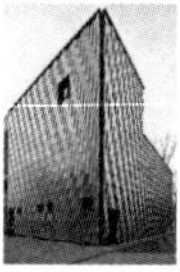

Heide & von Beckerath
① The many shades of gray (beyond others) ② Monochrome, translucent, or reflecting ③ It always depends on the material used
④ Recently visited: Le Corbusier's apartment-studio in Paris

Hobiger Feichtner Architekt*innen
① We'll take anything, as long as it's combined, but we especially like blue ② Smooth, glossy ceramic ③ Colored stains ④ Villa E-1027, Eileen Gray, inside

HOH Architecten
① Pastel Green (RAL 6019)
② Wall ③ Roller ④ Jardin Majorelle

Howland Evans Architects
① Red ② Marmoleum ③ Collage ④ Adolf Loos, Villa Müller

HPO
① Acid Green ② Human Skin
③ Texture Swap ④ Werner Tscholl, Selimex Headoffices

IMS Studio
① Dark blue ② Glossy
③ Varnish/enamel ④ House of Claude Monet

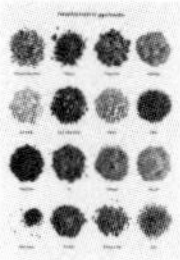

Institut für- gegen Baukultur
① RAL signal colors ② Worn/ patinated ③ Lubricate/ siliconize ④ /

Ivo Poças Martins
① Blue ② Wood ③ Sampling
④ La Muralla Roja, Ricardo Bofill

Johansen Skovsted Arkitekter
① Black green ② Saw-cut pine
③ Brush ④ Villa le Lac

JOUD VERGELY BEAUDOIN ARCHITECTES
① Natural colors ② Any surface required to enhance the character of a space
③ Associate color with raw materials and work on their appearance under light
④ Paimio Sanatorium, Alvar Aalto; Casa-Estudio, Luis Barragán

KAWAHARA KRAUSE ARCHITECTS
① Gold ② Assemblage
③ Fitting together small pieces
④ Nissei Theater, Togo Murano, 1963, Tokyo, Japan

Keßler Plescher Architekten
① Blush pink ② Wood
③ Japanese *urushi* ④ Villa Pestarini, Franco Albini

Klemen Breitfuss Architekt ETH
① This shade between the two NCS colors ② Ashwood
③ Trial and error ④ Verkehrsbauten Wiener Linien (Architektengruppe U-Bahn)

KOGAA
① Tangerine red ② Metal
③ Comaxit ④ Futurum by Kogaa

KOSMOS
① Functional ② Transparent
③ Handmade ④ Scaffolding in Valencia

Leeser Architecture
① Ice Blue ② Polished concrete ③ Casting ④ Unité d'Habitation de Marseille

MacIver-Ek Chevroulet
① Purple ② Skin
③ Galvanizing ④ Poul Henningsen's House

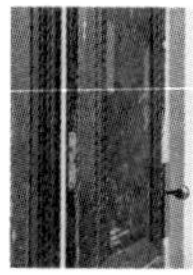

Mair-Paar Büro für Architektur
① The one that seizes you, even if you didn't expect it
② The one that just got you a splinter in your finger, but you don't care ③ The one that reveals layers and lets them shine ④ The one that creates its one definition of color, e.g., Atelier Rosa

Max Otto Zitzelsberger – Architekt BDA
① Himmelblau, Pantone 550
② Spiegelglatt ③ Lackierung
④ Eric Owen Moss, 708 house, Los Angeles

Meier Unger
① Light blue and almost blue/green-black ② Shiny glaze
③ Linseed oil ④ Aldo Rossi, Cabina d'Elba

Michael Maltzan Architecure
① Orange ② Medium density fiber board ③ Painted stucco ④ La Roche, Jeanneret house

Michael Reindel
① Neon yellow ② I am more interested in what lays behind the surface. The object or technique which holds the surface in position
③ Assemblage ④ House 43, architecten de vylder vinck taillieu

MONADNOCK
① IKB International Klein Blau ② Refelctive enameled panels, Villa Müller by Adolf Loos ③ FAUX ④ Pieter de Bruyne House

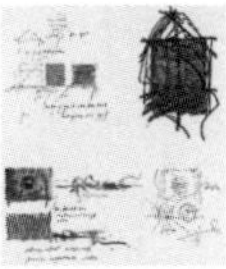

MRND
① RAL 6028 ② Concrete
③ Line drawing by pen on A4
④ Villa Furuholmen, Rå Arkitektur

Multerer Architekten
① Yellow ② Metal ③ Paint
④ Rietveld, Chauffeur's House

Muoto
① Blue ② Ribbed ③ /
④ Any Japanese house with blue tiled roof

Noreile Breen
① Warm and creamy; 24 carat yellow gold and pinks
② Chalky ③ Stucco
④ Sir John Soane's Museum, Lincoln's Inn Fields

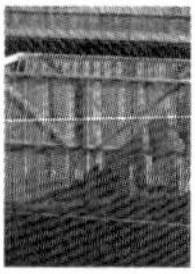

NOWADAYS office
① Color mix & match & overlay ② A surface that is not what it seems ③ Bricolage totalement ④ Our first project—a colorful pavilion

Nuno Melo Sousa
① Blue ② Walls ③ Pastels (dry oil) ④ Villa Sarabhai, Le Corbusier, Shahibag, India

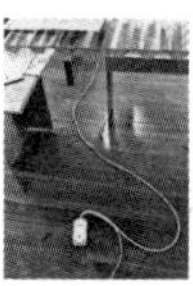

Office Kim Lenschow
① Wet room membrane blue ② Porous surfaces ③ Semi transparent coatings ④ House Rot Ellen Berg, Architecten De Vylder Vinck Taillieu

pablo saiz del rio + vivian rotie
① Matte ② Paper ③ Rammed earth ④ John Hejduk, Wall House 2

Point Supreme Architects
① Blue ② Patina ③ Hand-made ④ Frida Kahlo house

Present Forms
① Iridescence ② Butterfly wing ③ Animation ④ /

PROFFERLO Architecture
① RAL 5024 ② Metal sheet ③ Exposed material ④ Casa Balla, Via Oslavia, Rome

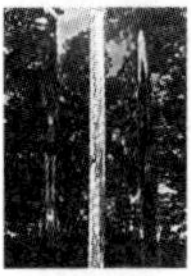

Sarah Naira
① Indecidable and always changing, depending on the mood ② Red hooded cars mirroring their surroundings and smooth sanded wood when warmed by the sun ③ Oil coloring ④ The blue floor tiles in the Glass House by Lina Bo Bardi reflecting the river flowing close to the plot (Sao Paulo); The House and Studio by Luis Barragan (Mexico City); or The Eames Case Study House by Charles and Ray Eames (Los Angeles).

Sauter von Moos
① Pink ② / ③ / ④ San Cristóbal

Schaub Zwicky Architekt:innen
① Blue ② Raw ③ Brushstroke ④ Moonraker Recreation Center, California

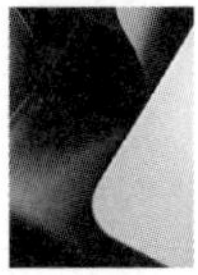

SCHNEIDER TÜRTSCHER
① Polychrome ② Ambiguous ③ Brushing ④ None

SET Architects
① Blue under the light ② Smooth steel ③ Spray paint ④ Maison La Roche-Jeanneret

Studio Andreas Lechner
① Rosso Rossi ② Plaster ③ Collage & montage ④ The Scholastic Building, Aldo Rossi; Morris Adjmi, New York 2001

studio eder krenn
① A6/C0 ② Aluminum ③ Anodize ④ Derek Jarmans's prospect cottage, including garden

Studio Eidola
① Earth tones (beige, terracotta, gray, brown) ② Imprint of the sand ③ Sand casting ④ We do not have any. In our work, colors are related to communication of the extraction site and the raw materials.

Studio Jakob Sellaoui
① Cardboard brown ② Cardboard ③ Good enough
④ Machiya in Minase, Kazunari Sakamoto, 1970

STUDIOLO
① Blue ② Polished marble
③ Stain painting ④ Villa Müller, Adolf Loos

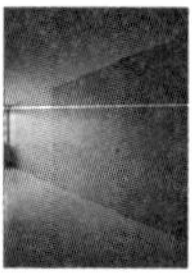

studiospazio
① The color of the environment ② Wood ③ Lacquering
④ Vernacular houses in Procida (IT)

SUJETS OBJETS/
① / ② Sagex ③ Drawing
④ Une Chambre en Ville, Dominique Gonzalez-Foerster, 1996

Theo De Meyer
① Depending on the surface and the technique ② Depending on the technique and the color ③ Depending on the surface and the color
④ Backyard

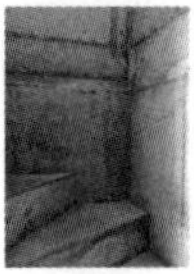

Wallimann Reichen
① Many. Even if they are incidental ② Combination of different surfaces and textures ③ / ④ Cuadra San Cristóbal, Luis Barragán

Wilhelm Scheruebl –
TAB collective
① Rainbow ② Screens
③ Falsification or Reality
④ Color Palace by Yinka Ilori and Pricegore

Exhibition

① Nuno Melo Sousa
② Michael Reindel
③ Institut Vierzehn
④ Nikola Hergovich
⑤ Luca Tommasi

Exhibition photographs:
Simon Oberhofer

⑤

④
⑤
①

⑤
①

①

Models

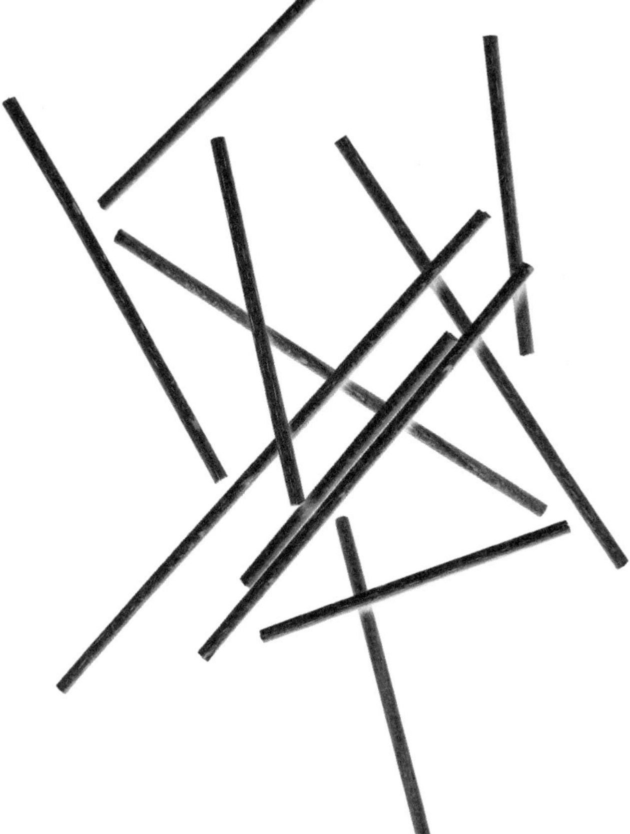

Diskursiv No. 1, Models

The dwindling appreciation for physical model-making in an era of digitalization is the problem that lies behind the first thematic focus, *Models*. This publication should be understood as a plea in favor of handcrafted model-making. Ever more realistic representations of planned projects—and with these, the design process—are made possible and accelerated by the progressive technologization of the architectural industry. Yet, this overrides a certain creative process that emerges through the physical confrontation with materials and the protracted time of engagement during the traditional model-making process.

Published by
Diskursiv, an association for
architectural research

ISBN 978-3-200-08550-3

Order here: info@diskursiv.xyz

Image Credits

Luca Tommasi
Fig. 1, © Koninklijke Bibliotheek, Den Haag, National Library of the Netherlands *Fig. 5*, © Kate Rothko Prizel and Christopher Rothko

Rafał Śliwa
Fig. 1, © Karl-Erik Olsson-Snogeröd *Fig. 2*, © Maxime Delvaux *Fig. 3*, © Karl-Erik Olsson-Snogeröd
Fig. 4, © Maxime Delvaux

Francesco Caneschi
Fig. 1, Courtesy of the Amsterdam Archive
Fig. 2, Courtesy of Gravalos Di Monte *Fig. 3*, © Ossip van Duivenbode *Fig. 4*, Comune di Milano *Fig. 5*, © Alessandro Imbriaco *Fig. 6*, © Agnese Morganti, Comune di Milano

Jan Engelke
Fig. 1: Schöner Wohnen 09/1968, p. 180–181
Fig. 2: Workshop colour specification Mercedes Benz
Fig. 3: Schöner Wohnen 09/1968, p. 178; photo by Maywald

HPO; Giorgio Scanelli and Riccardo Simioni
Fig. 2, © Louis De Belle

Franziska Hederer
Fig. 1: Philipp Otto Runge; in *Die Formen der Farben, Über Wechselwirkung der visuellen Elemente,* Karl Gerstner. Published by Athenaeum, Frankfurt 1986, p. 12.

Adam Sherman
Fig. 1-6, Courtesy of Jahn/

Paul Konrad
Fig. 1, © Philipp Schaerer
Fig. 2, © Charlotte Malterre-Barthes *Fig. 3*, The Royal Danish Academy, IBT, Cinark and Vandkunsten Architects
Fig. 4, © Per Eriksson
Fig. 5, © David Grandorge and Oskar Proctor *Fig. 6*, © David Grandorge and Oskar Proctor

Martin Grund and Wassily Walter
Fig. 1-4, © Oda Pälmke

Contributions #-Z

ATELIERDACOSTA, © Tiago Casanova *Atelier do Corvo,* © Maria Bicker *Atelier Starzak Strebicki,* © Danil Daneliuk *BELT,* © Alexander Gebetsroither *Bovenbouw Architectuur,* © Faaborg Museum by Hélène Binet *BUREAU,* © Dylan Perrenoud *Cierto Estudio,* © José Hevia *coabitare,* © David Schreyer

COCI, © Daniela & Tonatiuh *CORREIA/RAGAZZI ARQUITECTOS,* © Luis Ferreira Alves *Demo Working Group,* © Wolfgang Zeh *draftworks* architects,* © Creative Photo Room, Maria Efthymiou *Eagles of Architecture* © Filip Dujardin *Enrique Espinosa (Eeestudio) / Lys Villalba,* © José Hevia *EHRL BIELICKY,* © Scan by EHRL BIELICKY (original: Judith Turner photo of Peter Eisenmann House) *David Fink, Lukas Fink, Tobias Fink,* © Tobias Fink *Habsburg Isele Architekten,* © David Schreyer *Heide & von Beckerath,* © Andrew Alberts *HOH Architecten,* © Jordi Huisman *HPO,* © Louis De Belle *IMS Studio,* © wrschl. Architekten *Ivo Poças Martins,* © Attilio Fiumarella *JOUD VERGELY BEAUDOIN ARCHITECTES,* © Isabelle Bihr *Keßler Plescher Architekten,* © Carsten Pesch *KOGAA,* © Alex Shoots Buildings *Mair-Paar Büro für Architektur,* © wrschl. Architekten *Max Otto Zitzelsberger – Architekt BDA,* © Eric Owen Moss, 708 house, Los Angeles photo by Marvin Rand *Meier Unger,* © Lena Unger *MONADNOCK,* © Vandevorst, Kris *Multerer Architekten,* © Sebastian Schels/PK Odessa *Muoto,* © Maxime Delvaux *Noreile Breen,* © Alice Clancy and Noreile Breen *NOWADAYS office,* © Ilya Ivanov *Point Supreme Architects,* © Yannis Drakoulidis *PROFFERLO Architecture,* © Massimiliano Cafagna, Fabiana Dicuonzo *pablo saiz del rio + vivian rotie,* © Natalia Guardia *studiospazio,* © Karin Gauch, Fabien Schwartz *Theo De Meyer,* © Sybren Vanoverberghe

Imprint

© 2025 by jovis Verlag
An imprint of Walter de Gruyter GmbH, Berlin/Boston
Texts by kind permission of the authors. Pictures by kind permission of the photographers/holders of the picture rights.

All rights reserved.

Concept, editing, translation, and project management:
Diskursiv (Adna Babahmetović, Ajna Babahmetović, Julian Brües, Michael Hafner, Katharina Hohenwarter, Philipp Sternath)

Copy editing and proofreading:
Cecilia Tricker

Art direction and design:
A Gesture Of
(Simon Schindele, Simon Steinberger)

Project management jovis:
Charlotte Blumenthal

Lithography:
Bild1Druck, Berlin

Printing and binding:
KOPA, Lithuania

Bibliographic information published by the Deutsche Nationalbibliothek
The Deutsche Nationalbibliothek lists this publication in the Deutsche Nationalbibliografie; detailed bibliographic data are available on the Internet at http://dnb.d-nb.de

jovis Verlag
Genthiner Straße 13
10785 Berlin

www.jovis.de

jovis books are available worldwide in select bookstores. Please contact your nearest bookseller or visit www.jovis.de for information concerning your local distribution.

This book was printed with the kind support of

Bundesministerium
Kunst, Kultur,
öffentlicher Dienst und Sport

Das Land Steiermark
→ Kultur, Europa, Sport

GRAZ

TU Graz

(softcover)
ISBN 978-3-98612-136-5
(e-book)
ISBN 978-3-98612-137-2